T0328896

Customer Relationship Management (CRM) for Medium and Small Enterprises

Customer Relationship Management (CRM) for Medium and Small Enterprises

How to Find the Right Solution for Effectively Connecting with Your Customers

Antonio Specchia

Routledge
Taylor & Francis Group

A PRODUCTIVITY PRESS BOOK

First published 2022
by Routledge
605 Third Avenue, New York, NY 10158

and by Routledge
2 Park Square, Milton Park, Abingdon, Oxon, OX14 4RN

Routledge is an imprint of the Taylor & Francis Group, an informa business

© 2022 Antonio Specchia

ISBN: 9780367708894 (hbk)
ISBN: 9780367708863 (pbk)
ISBN: 9781003148388 (ebk)

DOI: 10.4324/9781003148388

Typeset in Garamond
by Deanta Global Publishing Services, Chennai, India

This book is dedicated to everyone who does not stop learning.

Contents

Foreword

It is refreshing in these times of "digital everything" to read a book that highlights the art and the profession of selling, through discussing CRM. We are, at least here in California, submerged by new products without a market and some of us don't go to pitching events anymore. VCs and angel investors are sick and tired of having to explain, to solitary inventors, that their opinions about their own products are useless without the evidence of a real market acceptability. Entrepreneurs, who count on their own personal likeability to raise capital, are in for a rude shock: they will be told that what really counts is not what one wishes to sell, but what people wish to purchase i.e. there is only one BOSS, the Market!

There is a legend that says Henry Ford disparaged the "customers". As he, apparently, had said that if he had asked the customers the answer would have been they wanted "faster horses"! He certainly had not asked the customers a thing because by age 46 he had gone bankrupt twice and it was only upon the establishing, under duress, of a proper advisory board and management team that the Ford Motor Company "invented" the modern car dealership concept, established 470 dealerships within the US and Canada, and started to sell automobiles like never before in history.

If producing cars is an art, selling them is also an art, together with financial management and controls; these three fields have to be executed equally well by passionate and competent practitioners who take pride in their specific professions. Marketing and sales are, however, more than a profession; they are the very essence of business.

- Products can be made for personal consumption, they can be someone's hobby or be invented and manufactured for personal enjoyment.
- Financial management without a transaction to account for would be non-existent.

■ But marketing and sales are the very essence of business, as expressed brilliantly by Peter Drucker: "The aim of business is to create and retain a customer".

The aim of any business, I teach, is not to make money! Making money is the outcome, the ultimate goal is to produce a product or service that adds value to the lives of others.

How to make people aware of your "solution" to their problem? How to find, reach, screen, inform, educate and interest possible users? What are the tools that strategic business developers use to research and identify potential clients? How to develop and maintain client relationships? How does one monitor project teams to ensure contracts are executed as agreed?

These are only some of the tasks of CRM that this book addresses. What really interests me is yet another aspect of the role of the "person who takes the product out of the company". I call these people the "marketers" and their best attribute, to me, is not that they sell the company's products as created. To me the real talent is that they "listen" to the feedback, the criticism, the real needs of the customers and have the chutzpah, the courage, to inform their "product people" about the real needs that the products DON'T fulfil. Since to be truly profitable the company has to offer a product/service that truly meets people' needs and satisfies what people want, the company's financial success cannot be reached without knowing, profoundly, its customers.

And this is the fundamental idea that makes me endorse, wholeheartedly, this book. If knowing yourself, according to Aristotle, is the beginning of wisdom, then knowing your customers, according to the author, is the very essence of business.

Ernesto Sirolli
Enterprise Facilitation founder, Sacramento CA

Why Entrepreneurs and Managers Should Read This Book

We believe that Customer Relationship Management (CRM) is a marketing challenge, not an IT matter. For this reason we want to offer an easy to digest book avoiding the excessive complexity of a fully comprehensive and too technical book—this book provides direct guidelines to those who need useful information on how to design and implement a CRM effectively, not in the operational way which is different by each tool, but in its logical structure: a logic that goes far and beyond the name of the vendor.

CRM is a growing topic among small and medium-sized enterprises as well as solopreneurs, and it is now clear that CRM is also a tool that businesses should have in place to manage sales processes. Teams of salespeople must have a system to run their daily activities, and small businesses and solopreneurs must have a way to track their marketing and sales effort, a functioning structure for maintaining their contacts with prospects and clients aimed to improve the effectiveness of their sales effort. CRM tools, once only available to large corporations, are now part of the powerful technology accessible also to small and medium businesses. Small and medium businesses are now able to implement CRM solutions with a more cost-effective balance as an alternative to traditional tools like Salesforce, Dynamics or Oracle. The reason for success is mainly the simplicity of the new tools and solutions that have been developed for the management of sales processes. This book discusses how to implement a CRM from the perspective of a business person—beyond the approach of IT consultants or technical staff—aiming to create benefits on the business development via enabling efficiency in Sales Management and setting a Sales Process control. Small and medium business owners may understand why and how implementing a CRM in its proper way will create value for the business—how it will boost business development by improving their sales management to lead to happier customers. Business professionals must be able to set up CRM systems avoiding mistakes and waste of time. This book provides an overview of what a CRM tool implementation should be able to enable in the organization and discusses the logic of CRM for sales management; essentially, it will give entrepreneurs the know-how behind CRM, supporting business to enhance their customers' relationship.

Acknowledgments

Thanks to many people this book is going to be real. I think they all know who they are—colleagues, friends, clients, experts, even those I only met once (or never)–with whom I shared ideas, and who inspired me.

I can mention CRM world gurus, to whom I had the opportunity to speak, and mentors who enabled me along the way.

The books in the Bibliography are there because I used them, I learnt from them and their authors. They all gave me something invaluable: knowledge.

I would like to mention people who helped me in this journey, like Liis Kupits and Elisa Turri, who both shared in the day-by-day effort during the book preparation. If there is ever a time that our paths go in different directions, I would say thank you for having been here with me for a while.

About the Author

I consider myself a businessman, my value proposition is CRM architect. It means my talent is to design and implement CRM, no matter which tool, according to the client's expectations. My job is to make the digital solution match the organisational requirements and the logic of its marketing strategy. I do this because of my marketing background and 20+ years of experience in marketing and sales. One consideration matters: even though I have written quite extensively and this is my second book on CRM, I'm a man of doing; I first consider what works, then why and how it works. Starting from that, I believe my approach to the CRM know-how can help everyone interested to learn more about the topic, especially those who are keen to use practical guides but also theoretical knowledge. My approach won't be too technical here; I'll use a logical approach, focusing on what actually works for business.

What I would like to achieve with this book is to inspire entrepreneurs and managers to use CRM in a more aware, confident and successful way, avoiding being sold a solution with incredible capability in theory, that is hard to use in practice. I want to help enable businesspeople to make better, informed decisions; to contract and lead service providers in a more effective way and, ultimately, set the organisational expectations on an effective knowledge of CRM logic.

I strongly believe that something hasn't been said enough: Customer Relationship Management is not at all an IT matter; CRM is, instead, first and foremost a marketing challenge! This is why I offer this book focusing on the logic of CRM and how it should work to support an organisational performance enhancement. In this sense, I can say that I *always start with why*.

Chapter 1

Understanding CRM

First of all I would like to make it clear that CRM is a marketing challenge and not at all an IT matter. This concept will be developed through the book, aiming to eliminate the confusion that we are just talking about software. While this is an introductory chapter, it is expected to provide an overview of the "Reason Why" and some background of the CRM.

For this reason the topics covered in this chapter are as follows:

- Introduction to the book
- About CRM
- Why so many people are not fully aware of what CRM is
- Introducing the concept of CRM
- The "Reason Why" of CRM
- Why CRMs tools are not all the same
- Our Idea of CRM
- How CRM became popular: a bit of storytelling
- The tool for Relationship Management
- Summary

Introduction to the Book

Choosing the appropriate software application to run Customer Relationship Management should be the outcome of an explicit organisational strategy, mainly about its purposes and how it should be deployed. The know-how to implement a CRM tool according to organisational strategy becomes critical to support the organisation's goals and achieve its objectives.

DOI: 10.4324/9781003148388-1

A well-implemented tool will help in executing the strategy for the best. Hence the capability to operate a decision about which tool, among the many available, should fit the organisation's needs while the way to implement it to support the organisational goals should also be part of the management know-how. For this reason, this book is not only about the process and techniques for setting up a tool, but it also presents various implications of the CRM and specifically its strong tie with an organisation's business strategy and the way it runs its marketing. Later in the book, we will see how to select software solutions and how they can be useful. In this chapter, we will start by analysing the logic of CRM and its connection with the business strategy.

As Paul Greenberg said, *"I do not use a CRM for myself, but as long as your business grows, you can reach a point where you can't even run your business without it."*[*]

About CRM (tool)

As you may already know, a CRM tool is just an application over databases. For that reason almost anyone can create a CRM, starting from scratch using any database (Db). The question is: *"...would the resulting CRM be any useful?"*[†] Hence, we may ask what exactly makes a solution usable for CRM purposes? Any Db is just a data container. Dbs differentiate themselves regarding Data Definition Languages, Speed, and Security. But what makes it usable for any specific purpose is the piece of software that lies between the human interaction and the Db, more than just the Db itself. Probably tech developers would have a slightly different opinion on this, but no one will deny the importance of the User Interface to boost the human interaction with the machine as an important element of the value of any digital solutions.

Thus, if you would like to develop a CRM over a simple Db you can surely do it, then you'd better be able to define functions and features in advance and set up the development of a proper software to manage the interface for users. This is why just using a spreadsheet as a CRM is not efficient, as we all now know.[‡]

---

[*] Greenberg, P., *The Godfather of CRM*, SalesPoP, 2019.
[†] Stephens, R., *Beginning Database Design Solution*, Wiley, 2009.
[‡] Koleda, E., *Why You Shouldn't Use a Google Sheet as a Database*, Medium, 2019.

What Makes CRM (tool) Useful

What really makes a CRM (tool) useful is the ability to track each interaction, task and communication with the contact persons bearing a clear and strong relationship to Opportunities and Companies related to that person. The CRM should capture every interaction easily, but on the other hand, users should be enabled to find out information within the whole track of the "relationship" with a person/organisation even more easily.

Again, the CRM tool should rely upon the concept of empowering our organisation to easily collect data around and about the people who interact with us as well as any interaction or opportunity that arises at any time with those people. And just the data that are truly useful for business purposes, not just any available or collectible data, should be uploaded in the tool. Collecting adequate data on a person's interests and needs enables the organisation that owns the CRM to use that data to shape information that can be useful to that person, to inform them about what matters to them and (ultimately) offer what he or she expects; doing this we create value to the organisation by pursuing its purposes. Finally, data can be truly powerful and useful when aggregated; the organisation then becomes capable of shaping information across market trends and business forecasts.

Why So Many People Are Not Fully Aware of What CRM Is

What remains unclear to many is what exactly a CRM is. Notwithstanding the growing importance of the tool and its rising popularity, if you ask for a definition of CRM and what it is useful for, rarely you will get a proper answer from managers or entrepreneurs.

Some random definitions of CRM you can come across could be:

> *"CRM ... refers to software that helps companies track interactions with their future and current customers."*
>
> ### *A Beginner's Guide to CRM*

> *"CRM is a way to identify, acquire, and retain customers, a business' greatest asset. Research has shown that companies that create satisfied, loyal customers have more repeat business, lower customer-acquisition costs, and stronger brand value, all of which translates into better financial performance."*
>
> ### *Siebel Systems*

"CRM is the process of managing interactions with existing as well as past and potential customers."

Insights Success

"CRM is the business strategy that aims to understand, anticipate, manage and personalize the needs of an organisation's current and potential customers"

PWC Consulting

"CRM is a strategy that companies use to manage interactions with customers and potential customers. CRM helps organisations streamline processes, build customer relationships, increase sales, improve customer service, and increase profitability.

When people talk about CRM, they are usually referring to a CRM system, a tool that is used for contact management, sales management, productivity, and more. The goal of a CRM system is simple: Improve business relationships."

Salesforce

"CRM means a combination of business strategies, software and processes that help build long-lasting relationships between companies and their customers"

Creatio

"CRM (is) an enterprisewide business strategy designed to optimize profitability, revenue and customer satisfaction by organising the enterprise around customer segments, fostering customer-satisfying behaviors and linking processes from customers through suppliers."

Gartner Group

*"CRM is all about understanding customers within the marketplace in order to meet and exceed their expectations, which will help achieve organisational objectives."**

Richard Bulton

---

* Bulton, R., *Creating and Managing a CRM Platform for Your Organisation*, Routledge, 2019.

Introducing the Concept of CRM

We can see how the idea of CRM as a system, just a digital tool, is largely in the minority amid those definitions. The most salient word among them is "strategy." It suggests that CRM is first and foremost a logic, an approach, a strategic view of the business and not just a software tool. And it makes sense as building relationships with customers is the essence of any business, the kernel of the recent developments in marketing. When the idea of marketing was conceptualised, the purpose was to crystallise a methodology around the interaction of businesses with markets. In its earliest version, Pete Borden's Marketing Mix that included the famous 4Ps,* showed his mainstream idea to leverage on policies to impact on markets and ultimately on each customer. Only 20 years later the American marketing scholars Leonard Berry and Barbara Jackson added a fresh theory about Relationship Marketing: While Berry argued that Relationship Marketing is a marketing activity to *"obtain, maintain and promote effective relationships with customers,"†* Jackson improved the concept of Relationship Marketing as a fresh new approach for the marketing industry. Her contribution focuses on the essence of Relationship Marketing which, according to her, is to *"attract, establish and maintain a close relationship with enterprise customers."‡*

> *"The aspect of long-term relationships with customers and other stakeholder groups has been neglected in mainstream marketing management literature, as pointed out by several scholars (Christopher et al., 1991; Dwyer et al., 1987; Ford, 1990; Grönroos, 1994b; Gummesson, 1997; Håkansson, 1982; Morgan and Hunt, 1994; Möller, 1992, 1994; Parvatiyar and Sheth, 1997; Sheth and Parvatiyar, 1995a)."§*

> *"...It has been welcomed as a saviour from the detrimental impact of traditional marketing or marketing-mix theory."¶*

---

* Borden, N. H., *"The Concept of the Marketing Mix,"* Journal of Advertising Research, 1964.
† Berry, L., *Relationship Marketing*. American Marketing Association, 1983.
‡ Jackson, B. B., *Winning and Keeping Industrial Customers*, Lexington Books, 1985.
§ Möller, K., Aino, H., *Relationship Marketing Theory: Its Roots and Direction*, Journal of Marketing Management, 2000.
¶ Grönroos, C., *From Marketing Mix to Relationship Marketing: Towards a Paradigm Shift in Marketing, Management Decision*, MCB UP Ltd., 1994.

This revamp of marketing as a collection of techniques to create, build and develop relationships with people* concurs with the vision of Thomas Siebel, the founder of Siebel Systems, which was the very first company focused on the development of a CRM system as a digital tool. We could say that in the 90's we saw "Relationship Marketing" giving birth to CRM software to execute marketing strategies. The transactional marketing paved the way to a new approach where transactions were consequences of relationships with stakeholders, and specifically with clients.†

"Reason Why" of CRM

With this picture in mind we can now better understand CRM in its whole scope, spanning well beyond the simple "keep in touch with clients" and including the whole marketing process, especially in its sales stage. More than customers we should perceive clients as persons, eventually stakeholders, who are each situated at different stages of a relationship with the company. From ignorance and unawareness, to an aware interest (or aware lack of interest), to repeat customers, they all have a type of relationship—from none to close—that matters to the business.

> *"Companies large and small across a variety of sectors are embracing CRM as a major element of corporate strategy for two important reasons: new technologies now enable companies to target chosen market segments, micro-segments or individual customers more precisely and new marketing thinking has recognized the limitations of traditional marketing and the potential of more customer-focused, process-based strategies."‡*

From Policies to People

Probably the biggest shift from managing policies to managing relationships can be approximated by two opposite approaches:

---

* Christopher, M., Payne, A., Ballantyne, D., *Relationship Marketing: Creating Shareholder Value*, Butterworth-Heinemann, 2002.

† Kotler, P., *It's time for total marketing,* Business Week Advance Executive Brief, 1992.

‡ Payne, A., *Handbook of CRM*, Butterworth-Heinemann, Elsevier-Routledge, 2005.

- Policies are enacted and their outcomes are checked so that they can be altered, struck out or confirmed.
- Policies are designed over market understanding, generally based on relevant group segments analysis.
- Relationships are created using messages and contents, by engaging people on a more direct, often at the personal level.
- Relationships are built and developed, while feedbacks are tracked, as relationships can end, stagnate, continue or thrive.

The informative power of direct relationships with people who can or can't be customers is deeper and more detailed than just measuring policies outcomes.

Why CRM Tools Are Not All the Same

The previous conceptualisation seeks to clarify the enormous difference between the two main types of business models: consumer oriented and company oriented, also known as business-to-consumer (B2C) and business-to-business (B2B) models. We believe that this dichotomy between B2C and B2B also impacts on the CRM as a choice between employable tools, while probably it matters with regard to applicable marketing strategies. One can define B2C as aimed at a large number of clients, with little or no relevant value per single transaction. On the other hand, B2B is generally characterised by smaller audiences but significant values per transaction. The difference between the two models is also related to the usefulness of Relationship Marketing: while in B2B each person counts and each single relationship matters, in B2C the focus is not so much on each single person, even if the effort to make each client "feel good" is still important. Hence when we evaluate B2B, Relationship Marketing really matters whereas when we discuss B2C, Relationship Marketing takes a different path.

To understand CRM as a strategic approach or even as a tool, we will divide these two perspectives into two specific discussions when required, even though they have a strong common basis that often converge, as boundaries are not set in stone. Thus some techniques and methodologies from B2B can blend into a more people-oriented approach. We will discuss each point later in detail.

Our Idea of CRM

Our idea of CRM should be clear by now: it is the logic that influences brand's marketing on long-term decisions and ultimately, the way in which the company operates on the market. At the same time, CRM is also the tool used to manage the company's presence in the markets and its interactions with stakeholders.

We see the CRM as the link between marketing strategy and marketing processes, the way to manage the execution of the company's mission on a daily basis. It is a concept that functions as the strategic attitude (CRM logic), but it is also a real thing: the software that empowers the organisation in executing strategies (CRM tool).

> *"...What has changed over the past decade(s) is a series of significant trends that collectively shape the opportunity to better serve customers through information-enabled relationships marketing, or CRM."*

How CRM Became Popular: A Bit of Storytelling

Companies can get the same CRM results using just pencil and paper. Nobody today recalls that the first method for keeping in touch with clients was a Rolodex, just a repository of names and main data. Later came the time of business cards book.

Some companies see less value in any complex system for tracking clients' interactions; this is logical when the business model is focused on very few clients, or even only one, and everything is managed manually by one or two persons. As soon as we see a shift away from those circumstances and the number of clients rises, so too does the changeover of clients, then keeping track of interactions manually becomes more difficult.

In the early 2000s, Salesforce promoted themselves with a strong message to compete with strong existing players: what should be, what is now, and how to close the gap. In a few statements Salesforce highlighted their Unique Selling Proposition.

---

* Payne, A., *Handbook of CRM*, Butterworth-Heinemann, Elsevier-Routledge, 2005.

A Salesforce Advertising Message in Its Early Stage*

> Heaven is where business' operations and infrastructure are Efficient and Effective
>
> Hell is where operations are stuck, infrastructure are slow or broken and the effort to achieve anything is excessive
>
> Sin is to buy software from companies like Oracle and Siebel that are expensive and inefficient
>
> Correct shift is to use software as a service, and letting the service by a provider that can manage it efficiently on behalf of you
>
> Namely ending the software ownership (reducing CapEx)

If this message was real, and we believe it was, the implication is interesting. We can see the disruptive approach that Salesforce took against such huge players.[†]

What was promised by Salesforce's CRM was a smooth process management that would boost the business; what was being delivered by the bigshots at the time were often hugely expensive, sometimes ineffective solutions that took businesses to the ground (clients said). But we were then only in the early stage of CRM evolution.

A Disruptive Approach

Salesforce moved the greatest part of the software development out of clients' offices—and ownership—enabling clients to access a platform. This disruptive approach has shown its benefits on a technical level as well as at the financial level. It gave a strong boost to markets by reducing costs and raising performance. In the first decade of this century, Salesforce recorded a fantastic growth rate, hitting US$1.6 billion in turnover, then continued growing also in the second decade at outstanding rate: they hit US$20 billion in 2020 (to be fair, acquisitions along the way comprise a big part of this turnover growth). Around 2010, more solutions started appearing on the market but demand grew even faster, creating space for many players. Some major players were established before 2010; SugarCRM was founded in 2004 and Hubspot in 2006, even if their growth didn't soar as much as Salesforce did, they are still relevant players among the plethora of contenders. Last year the

---

* Unknown source.

† Kellogg, D., *Is Salesforce/Siebel a Classic Disruption Case?*, Kellblog, 2014.

solutions available on the market numbered more than 600 different players, and still growing.

Well Beyond Numbers

But the market numbers are only the visible side of the phenomenon and they reflect the trend of organisations that approached CRM tools in the hope of gaining efficiency in their processes. What developed clearly in the last ten years is a growing interest around the topic, more literature, a wider embrace by companies; generally a growing awareness of the benefits of the digital solution for the business. The growth in demand has led directly to the growth in the solutions offered.

The Leader Is Here to Stay

If Salesforce's role as leader of the industry has been clear, and its position appears even stronger nowadays, the widening of demand has given many competitors the opportunity to enter a lucrative market. And thanks to new available technologies that have given newcomers the possibility to become more efficient, smarter and faster than the old giant, the industry appears to be in turbulence even now. It is not foreseeable whether the leader will be overthrown, but there is certainly remarkable growth happening lower down in the industry.

The stronger trends among the contenders seem to be two, namely sales process management and marketing automation, while customer service and call centres remain relevant but less trendy. The two features are often related to CRM tout-court; in fact they are two stages of CRM in general, but the proposition focus mainly upon one of them. Another important trend involves off-the-shelves (or pre-built) platforms versus more customisable solutions, where pre-built platforms are cheaper and (theoretically) easier to adopt especially for small businesses; they answer to the demand from new users giving the whole industry a significant boost.

More Market, More Options, More Opportunities

Nowadays organisations have a variety of options available in the market at almost any price, but most importantly they can choose among many different approaches and ways to solve the problem. Such availability can lead to a better match between the company's expectations and the tool, even if the selection process can be more confusing and time consuming. Companies that find the right solution reveal good financial reports,* to prove that the trend is here to stay and that it is healthy for businesses, customers and employees as well.

An Innovation That Matters for Every Business

Markets change at a really fast pace; clients are more complex to retain, margins shrink, and competition becomes harder as new, cheaper technologies become available and empower small businesses to compete with big players.

Companies today can seek to improve their customer management by utilizing a range of database, data mart and data warehouse technologies, as well as a growing number of CRM applications. Such developments make it possible to gather vast amounts of customer data and increase customer feedback, as well as to analyse, interpret and utilize them constructively. Furthermore, the advantages presented by increasingly powerful computer hardware, software and e-services are augmented by the decreasing costs of running them. This plethora of available and more affordable tools of CRM is enabling companies to target the most promising opportunities more effectively.† We would add that companies seek efficiency by implementing digital transformation, doing more with fewer resources in order to create a competitive advantage. CRM systems should first focus on the real improvement of operational efficiency in any processes managed, and should then proceed to discuss the return on investment (ROI) of the possible solutions, as efficiency enhancement is directly related to better financial performance.

The Tool for Relationship Management

As we said at the beginning of this chapter, a CRM tool technically is just a database empowered with some specific functions by an overlaying software. The Db performances are important as they can affect the system performance. Imagine a CRM that takes 15 seconds to give you access to information; it would be considered not acceptable. Mainly the user

---

* Leggett, K., *Quantify The Business Value of CRM*, Forrester Research, 2019.
† Payne, A., 2005, ibid.

experience, including lead time, often gets more relevance in the software that manages the Db rather than the Db performances.

But let's consider this: *"A database is a tool that stores data, and lets you create, read, update, and delete the data in some manner."** While according to the definition of CRM seen before, we can define the CRM as an organisational activity to develop the knowledge about markets and stakeholders.

This organisational function can be performed by a CRM tool, which is a platform or a software designed to instil efficiency specifically in this part of the human labour. Like any data storage the tool is *a system to process, maintain and retrieve transactional, behavioural, personal and social data in the most efficient way*. The purpose is to create effective, meaningful information arrays, available in real time, fulfilling organisational needs and supporting the achievement of the company's mission.

Among the expected features we can list:

- providing information to support marketing activities—campaigns, events, communication to specific audiences, etc.;
- enabling companies to preside over multiple contacts (leads), understand individuals' and organisations' needs, qualify potential customers by proper parameters;
- enabling market analysis and understanding by highlighting tendencies and growing needs through individuals' and organisations' feedback tracking;
- supporting sales processes, deploying execution of activities related to each designed sales stage along the sales process journey; and
- enabling sales process management by reporting over sales process efforts and results, thereby aiding forecast management and sales process planning.

The specific purposes of a CRM tool are to:

- Ignite efficiency in the organisational collection of data, assembling more reliable information about individuals and organisations to hit marketing goals
- Ignite efficiency in sales process management to boost sales effectiveness

---

* Stephens, R., *Beginning Database Design Solutions*, Wiley, 2009.

■ Provide data into the organisational infrastructure enabling meeting business objectives

Over this conceptual framework we can list many features that a system can or has to allow to users; we normally incorporate them in four big areas:

1. Leads Generation
2. Sales
3. Customer Service
4. Operations

These areas of intervention embrace the whole business; just adding some features like project management and process management, we would be depicting a system that can create the backbone of the whole company. By gathering data from different sources and offering them, in real time, to data's consumers, the system can effectively substitute several data silos that companies are used to run.

Now it should be clearer how the CRM function is much more than just contacting clients.

CRM Big Bang, or Not

Companies can activate all functions at once or just select some of them and start from there, adding other features later in a phased manner. In the meantime, different platforms can arise more focused (and useful) on one area than another, creating the opportunity to shift from one to another, while the big picture would eventually lead to a fully integrated system that can virtually connect any process in the business. We can argue about whether such a complex system is something to launch as a single big event, an all-in-one shot, or if it should be built in stages, seeking outcomes by nurturing a learning-by-doing process. We will analyse each such prospect in the second chapter of this book, but we must acknowledge that technology changes fast and the procedure that was formerly used to build complex, all-in-one tools by a well-established and verified provider is not a must anymore.

Summary

In this chapter we introduced CRM in general.

- We discussed the logic of CRM well beyond its scope as digital tool, but mainly its role related to business strategy execution.
- We discussed what a CRM tool is, having started by looking at what a database is.
- We also discussed CRM as a marketing revamp that influenced the industry immensely and how the subsequent digital revolution enabled the creation of the CRM digital tool.
- Then we discussed how it became widely adopted in organisations and what value it brings to them.

Chapter 2

The Value for the Organisation

Hundreds of customer relationship management (CRM) software pro-grammes are today available in the market; they respond to a growing demand mainly led by small and medium-sized enterprises (SMEs). Lately the competition has been high and it can be complex to understand the value each tool can create for an organisation. To simplify the problem we will evaluate the benefits that a CRM can generate for an organisation and in the last chapter of this book we will go through some different platforms to evaluate their approaches. In this chapter, the focus will be on the value that the adoption of a CRM system can create for any organisation in its gen-eral approach. To evaluate what and how each company would be able to extract value is a more critical point: to support the understanding that each company should run upon their own situation, better to check case history of medium-size companies later in this book.

The topics covered in this chapter are as follows:

1. Digital transformation for whom
2. CRM is a journey, not an event: a Lean Approach
3. CRM project success
4. Process-Data-Driven architecture
5. Multichannel interaction
6. Value creation
7. Performance assessment
8. Summary

DOI: 10.4324/9781003148388-2

Digital Transformation for Whom

The approach to develop digital solutions is generally more mature in large enterprises, while medium and small businesses find it more difficult to develop a long-term approach to digital transformation. It has been said that management tends to overestimate the short-term benefits of digital investments while they are keen to underestimate the long-term benefits of digitalisation. It probably speaks to a human tendency to lower expectations upon long-term value of everything in general. What we can count on is here and now, while what will happen in years to come is out of sight.

But corporations are not infallible. Accenture, in their report *"Digital Value or Digital Vanity,"* states:

> *"It is hard to believe that any company would invest millions in a major transformation without a clear picture of the value delivered. Yet this is happening every day when it comes to digital. Not only is it the hottest investment around, it is the most difficult to quantify."**

If this is what corporations do, how would medium and small businesses be any different? The literature usually points out that actually small companies are less capable to benefit from digitalisation and they are slower in seeking the productivity enhancement related to digital transformation at any level. It is commonly reported how corporations can leverage productivity enhancement on a larger scale, and that creates a significant incentive for them to invest in digital transformation.

On the other hand, we experience the complex world of medium and small businesses on a daily basis, and we tend to agree with many authors' voices when they report: *small is beautiful.*† Some authors highlight the benefit of starting businesses small and making them grow;‡ some just focus on the smallest scale of business as possibly being the most human friendly;§ while others point out that the bigger a business is, the worse it works.¶ But even without fully embracing the pessimistic view of Freek Vermeulen, we

---

* Campagna, C., Arora, S., Delawalla, A., *Accenture-Digital-Value-POV-V05-FINAL.pdf*, https://www. accenture.com/_acnmedia/pdf-77/accenture-digital-value-pov-v05-final.pdf Accenture, 2018.
† Schumacher, E. F., *Small Is Beautiful*, Vintage Publishing, 1973.
‡ Sirolli, E., *How to Start a Business & Ignite Your Life*, Square One Publishers, 2012.
§ Jarvis, P., *Company of One: Why Staying Small Is the Next Big Thing for Business*, Houghton Mifflin Harcourt, 2019.
¶ Vermeulen, F., *Business Exposed, The Naked Truth about What Really Goes on in the World of Business*, Pearson, 2010.

can recognise that big corporations are not the heaven, and yet they play a paramount role in our society.*

There is a pervasive belief that medium-sized companies have a vital role in our society in maintaining social cohesion, spreading innovation and managing resources even better than big corporations can do,† if for no other reason than that they just can't afford to waste millions of dollars.

This is not the right space to fully discuss this topic, but let's say that one of the large corporations' main innovation strategy is based on acquiring start-ups and small businesses that have been able to ignite great ideas and bring them to life. This is something that bigger organisations find hard to achieve. At the same time, medium and small businesses dramatically out-number large corporations, and a tremendous amount of innovation happens in SMEs.‡

We should therefore discuss how medium and small businesses are not only able to benefit from the digital revolution, as they are the first utilisers of innovations put in place by High Tech corporations, but they actually are also the real engine of innovation, creating it and applying it to many areas of human life.§

CRM Is a Journey, Not an Event

Innovation, and particularly digital transformation, in each of its denotations, is often seen as a disruptive shift, usually perceived as a change of paradigm from manual human-based work to embracing machine-driven production.

If we take this view, we should consider that digital transformation began in large scale in the 90's and is still here. Even companies that started embracing "digitalisation" early on are still involved in continuous technological improvement. They have spent 25+ years developing their own "digital being", making this not just a transformation, but a different existential paradigm where being digital is the way to exist. Hence digital transformation (DT) is clearly not an

---

* Baumann, H. D., *Building Lean Companies: How to Keep Companies Profitable as They Grow*, Morgan James Publishing, 2009.

† European Commission, *Entrepreneurship and small and medium-sized enterprises (SMEs)*, [https://ec.europa.eu/growth/smes_en].

‡ United Nation Conference on Trade and Development, *Why we should care more about small and medium-sized enterprises*, 2016 [https://unctad.org/news/why-we-should-care-more-about-small-and-medium-sized-enterprises].

§ Acs, Z., Carlsson, B., Karlsson, C., *Entrepreneurship, Small and Medium-Sized Enterprises and the Macroeconomy*, Cambridge University Press, 1999.

event; it has better depicted itself as a journey. But probably it will soon be clear that there is no end to that journey: digitalisation is a long-term continuous adjustment that includes fine tuning, alteration and, not rarely, complete changes of methods. It is clearly not just something to put in place and go.

In the same way, when an organisation embraces a project over CRM, either to perform a completely new instalment over a blank slate or to implement a new tool to substitute the existing one, they should be aware of the long-term process that needs to be run so that they can begin to build it from the very first step. Defining the strategy and figuring out how to execute it will be the first stage that frees the organisation from just embracing the tool as a "way-to-do." Companies should be aware of how a gradualistic approach enables them to adjust the next steps over each stage's outcome; it is powerful. If we were to seek a metaphor to explain the CRM implementation project to anyone who is familiar with the lean start-up approach,* we could utilise that method to better explain how to engage with a CRM implementation process: start small, test, learn, improve. An approach that, ultimately, is extremely useful to any digital matter, while it could be less valuable for other, more bricks and mortar, circumstances.

This approach implies a clear vision and understanding of the long-term result you aim to achieve. Then the how, that is the execution tactics, will be something you put in place according to the long-term vision. Developing a clear understanding of CRM as a know-how, a strategy, and over the management of tools that can facilitate it, will enable you to stick with the execution of the strategy even if the tool changes. It enables you to become independent from specific "way-to-do" that each tool may impose. Empowering the organisation to govern the execution by choosing the tool that properly fits the organisational requirements instead of being driven by the tool's way-to-do, with limited or no plan for the strategy, that would trap you in the tool.

A list of milestones on that journey would reveal two main areas, namely strategy and execution. Starting with the first area of CRM, strategy, we would investigate:

- The reason why relationships are (would be) important for your business
- The different (possible) lifetime value of the different types of clients
- What transitional marketing strategies did your business leverage

---

* Ries, E., *The Lean Startup*, Crown Business, 2011.

■ How a transition to relationship marketing would transform the inside culture
■ What cross-functional approach would be good
■ How to flex the organisation to a new paradigm
■ Why this shift would be relevant in the competitive environment
■ How messages engage leads and what should be the promise of the business in a relationship marketing paradigm
■ How to boost the service culture of the organisation
■ How to inspire the sales culture to place customers at the centre of business
■ How to embrace a value proposition based on trustworthiness
■ How sales should happen and what the outcomes should be
■ How the new business should take place, where the new people could be found and why they would come to you
■ How the organisation could shift into a one-to-one marketing paradigm

The previous list can probably be extended according to the organisation's circumstances. It is important to investigate the brand's character; the business "reason-why" that will enable the organisation to highlight the strategic matter. Clarify how the would-be (if not already begun) transition from a traditional marketing approach (and behaviours), mainly transactions-oriented, to a paradigm of people-centred and relationship-based engagement would enable the organisation to survive.

On the other hand, regarding how to execute the CRM implementation, we would enlist more actionable tasks:

■ What processes would be the priority for enhancement by a digital tool
■ How processes should work according to the RM
■ How new prospects engagement should work
■ How nurturing existing clients should work
■ How upsales to existing clients should work
■ How cross-selling to existing and potential clients should work
■ What a prospect thinks, sees, says, feels
■ What is the pain, and how does he/she have been solving it
■ How the value proposition would better be recognised by potential clients
■ What are the activities to be done alongside the sales process
■ How service should be delivered before and after sales

- What is right to know, understand and test regarding prospects' decision making
- What user experience competitors offer in their product/services mix
- How the users/clients' expectation will rise over time.

The preceding list includes more actionable tasks; however, it is not exhaustive but a mere trail to lead a deeper analysis aimed to clarify within the organisation, understanding the purposes and prepare for the CRM implementation.

It should be clear that, although we are only at the beginning of the plan, and without having considered the technical aspects of the deployment, we can already foresee how many of the topics in the previous lists are dynamic.

When parameters change, the execution should follow suit, and without listing each of them you can immediately predict how the changes in some of them would have a relevant effect on managed processes. If the processes need to be adapted, the CRM tool, as a system, should be able to facilitate it. Although many tools could be flexible enough to follow organisational adjustments, what does really matter here is to clarify the complexity by crystallising a system design and putting it in place in one shot.

It could be intuitive how a lean approach would help in adapting to new circumstances, but too often the myth of saving resources with a big bang leads managers to forget the benefits of lean methodology.

CRM Project Success

Formulating a proper definition of CRM is not just a workout of words and concepts affecting just minds; the way we define CRM will impact how the organisation will perceive it and what expectations it will exert. The definition itself affects how CRM is accepted and practised in daily routines. *"It involves a profound synthesis of strategic vision, a corporate understanding of the nature of customer value within a multi-channel environment."** Payne and Frow suggest a continuum between the dichotomic definitions of CRM: the logical, strategic matter on one side and the technological solutions on the other.† We agree with that graphic explanation of the perception that

---

* Payne, A., *Handbook of CRM*, Routledge, 2005.
† Payne, A., Frow, P., *A strategic framework for customer relationship management*. Journal of Marketing, 2005.

organisations exhibit about CRM. We can add that probably in the last 15 years, all those organisations that took the strategic perspective on CRM are, unfortunately, at risk of extinction.

In fact, CRM project failure hasn't slowed down since Adrian Payne reported an astonishing 70% failure rate for CRM implementation projects in 2005. Recent studies cite a project failure rate of up to a daunting 90%!* Another author lowered the failure rate to just 70%, stating clearly the reason: *"It is expected that the system itself will bring the content and strategic direction for marketing, sales and service. However, a system can only map and structure strategic content, but cannot create it."†* Hence, we live in an odd situation in which CRM adoption is booming, with more and more companies asking for it, but the industry is failing to deliver the expected results.

Clearly, the dichotomic model described by Payne and Frow helps to show managers' perception of CRM. A model that would better describe the reality of the paradigm would show technological solutions embedded in the strategic approach, as both are necessary; the tool can only create value under the strategic umbrella (Figure 2.1), in the absence of which failure is guaranteed.

Process Data-Driven Architecture

Although CRM enables organisations to collect data, what organisations do with that data can often be cloudy. To outline what it means to be a process-driven as opposed to a function-driven organisation, let's imagine the customer journey. A stakeholder perceives the organisation as singular being, one single entity; the functional boundaries are in place to support the sharing of duties and responsibilities over stages of the client's continuous journey, improving the productivity of employees. In Figure 2.2, the customers are the receivers of outputs of organisational functions. The main goal, from the customer-centric point of view, would be to make them perceive the unity of the organisation even if they interact with different people. Then there are internal processes:

■ Strategy development
■ Value definition

---

* Edinger, S., *Why CRM Projects Fail and How to Make Them More Successful*, HBR, 2018.
† Guethoff, A., *Why 70% of all CRM projects fail … and how yours will not be one of them*, LinkedIn, May 2020.

Figure 2.1 CRM tool as the kernel of strategic thinking.

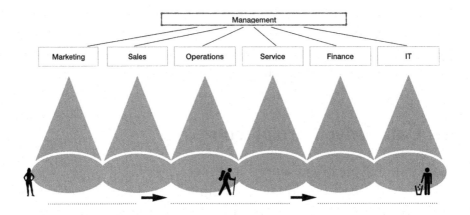

Figure 2.2 Functional organisation.

- ■ Information management
- ■ Multichannel interaction
- ■ Value creation
- ■ Performance assessment

Internal processes consume data. They gather data about markets, customers, competitors, stakeholders, and events to elaborate information used to propel decision-making. Data that become available in each functional area are collected, and they are related, to the same customer or stakeholder. The customer-centred approach not only matters in terms of customer experience but also impacts on data management, being able to track events along the way as well as decisions taken consequently. All this portrays the customer journey and the experiences related to it (Figure 2.2).

The processes enumerated above belong to two domains, namely strategic and operative. Strategic processes comprise the first three bullet points, while multichannel interaction, value creation and performance assessment are more operational. We will discuss the operational ones here.

Multichannel Interaction

The number of channels for communication have proliferated in the last decade, and many of them have become ordinary media for business communication as well as personal interactions. Voice communication is becoming more and more important lately as the fast pace of today's life requires faster interactions and more efficient ways of exchanging information. In today's business-to-consumer (B2C) environment, contracts are often finalized by voice interaction, and while e-mail has been the biggest shift from paper communication, today the relevance of that media is shrinking. Thus the need to govern more channels, not only to be reached but also to give information and collect data, becomes central in the digital transformation journey. WhatsApp, for instance, is becoming important and, increasingly after the acquisition by Facebook, is relevant as a direct, personal contact media. This also boosts Messenger from Facebook; for every company that has a Facebook page, Messenger matters.

Voice rendering is also growing in focus, especially on mobile devices, as it can drive interactions with customers in many cases, ranging from the engagement of new clients to customer service.

Value Creation

While value definition is a strategic endeavour, the creation, or even better the co-creation of value, belongs to the front line, or the operational sphere. The utility value is a relevant conceptualisation for business, and it also implies discussion of the so-called value trade-off: customers should receive a valuable usefulness from the product/service provided to justify the trade, and that value has to be higher than the corresponding value they could receive using alternative solutions. That higher value proposed should cost (the producer) a fraction of the cost that customers would face when utilising different methods. The difference between value perceived and cost of production is the value extracted from the client. Or, better, it is the area where the producer decides to place its price: the higher the price, the greater the margin that can be extracted from the clients; the lower the price, the greater the value that will be delivered to the client (that can also backfire).

But what matters is how organisations can effectively master their influence on the value perceived. In this domain, it probably relies on the most important part of relationship marketing. If transactional marketing was based on a massive communication to audiences who then would decide their preferences, relationship marketing relies on a more complex process to nurture customer preferences. The back-and-forth between clients and organisations, the several interactions that happen along the way, even more than the still important moment of truth,* shape the client's experience and affect their preferences. For this very reason, relationship marketing places the client's experience under a crucial perspective, and at its best a continued, positive relationship is the best influencer of customer preferences.[†]

By now it is clear how CRM as a postulate boosts the customisation of the value creation process. This process is even more relevant in B2C environments where sometimes prices emerge alongside the relationship itself. Value, and thus price, is a matter of perception rather than cost, the relationship is the territory where perception is created, developed and nurtured, but also negotiated between different perspectives.

As mentioned, the CRM tool's role is to support CRM logic; it means also to facilitate the clarity of value proposition to the clients along the sales journey. So it will be possible to outreach the value co-creation.

Performance Assessment

Information technology firmly dominates this area of organisational management. In a new paradigm of people-centred events and data-driven processes, there is no concern that a cross-process repository that empowers efficiency in processes and interactions may enable a gentle assessment of performance.

Activities and tasks related to customers along the relationship are part of the labour required to run the business, sometimes the greatest chunk of

---

* Gröonros, C., *Service Management and Marketing*, Lexington Books, 1990.
[†] Foxall, G. R., *Consumer Behaviour Analysis: The Behavioural Basis of Consumer Choice*, Routledge, 2002.

it. Measuring and planning the effort empowers in planning improvements, fostering efficiency in processes and in the business as a whole. This definitively exerts influence on the bottom line.

A CRM can become the daily tool for many processes related to interaction with clients. If featured with activities tracking, the CRM can enable reporting of cumulative tracking as well as individual activities. Both can be useful to assess process effort as the amount of work required against the results per deal, per salesperson and cumulatively. The amount of work required for creating the service with clients, especially during the sales process, has always been under debate and it is commonly considered hard to measure and even harder to plan with accuracy.

While in other processes we can better relate activities to results, in sales processes and also in processes that affect people in general, this can be quite varied and often hard to track. But very often it's where the greatest potential for enhancement can be hidden, and developing a gentle way to track activities can unleash productivity enhancement.

Summary

In this chapter, we analysed the digital transformation for medium and small businesses, why it happens and what aspects of it matter to them.

- We highlighted the role of medium businesses in stimulating innovation and their role in the economy.

We clarified once more how CRM is mainly a strategic matter, and only later a technological tool, software being the support for execution of the strategy.

- CRM tools come later; first comes the strategy of Relationship Marketing.

We analysed what specifically about CRM implementation is part of the digital transformation and gave a general overview of the reason why implementation projects should be considered long-term projects and not one-off.

- Hence, it is important to carefully consider the rate of project failure as a warning before fully embracing the implementation.

We then described how data-driven processes dominate the organisations and how a CRM tool would allow better control of them.

■ Management decision-making is a net "data consumer" to be fed continuously.

We then evaluated three operational processes that are strongly related to CRM, and how they can be included in and boosted by CRM as a tool.

■ As they are directly involved with execution processes, they can directly show the value created by implementing the CRM tool.

Chapter 3

Sales Process Management

At its beginning, customer relationship management systems were developed mainly for customer care/services purposes. This usage was firstly developed by Thomas Siebel, and it was CRM's main purpose till the first decade of this century when the technology started gaining more popularity in the sales departments of medium businesses in business-to-business (B2B) markets. Today among medium and small businesses that implement CRM, almost all of them aim to enhance the sales process management. This shift into the revenue-generating area could be among the reasons that have boosted the demand for CRM technology.

In this chapter, we will describe the secrets of CRM for sales process management and how to implement it.

The topics covered in this chapter are as follows:

- Sales process design
- Sales process stages
- Lead-in
  - Contacting
- Discovery opportunities
- Qualification
  - Qualification methods
  - Qualification purpose and outcome
  - Developing solutions
  - Negotiation
- Learning opportunity
- Purpose and outcome

DOI: 10.4324/9781003148388-3

Sales Process Design

The sales job has always been considered unpredictable by definition. And it is still beyond direct control: even the most successful salespersons are able to win only a slice of all the opportunities they come across. At least in normal conditions, in my country we have a motto with regard to sales: *you can fool one person all the time or everyone once, but you can't fool everyone all the time.** The logic is clear: we can't control other people's decisions; we can try to influence them and we can become very convincing using the art of persuasion,† but we cannot drive them to decide. Luckily nobody really can control it. We can see this also by analysing what the best salespeople do: they provide a well-structured, informative "service" that leads their counterparts through a planned experience. The more that experience fits the buyer's expectations, the more it is that likely a positive closure will be reached.

In this chapter, we refer mainly to the business-to-business approach, while the business-to-consumer sector often, though not always, has simpler sales processes. In the real estate domain, for instance, the sales process for private families is generally not that simple and fast. This suggests that it is not so much the wider B2B or B2C scheme that matters when it comes to the complexity of sales processes, but that they largely depend on the kind of purchase and on whether buyers perceive the service/product as a commodity or, instead, as something mission-critical.

But how exactly does the "sales process" work? It could seem odd if while designing a CRM we ask clients to explain their sales processes and they are stuck in a moment of silence. Even well-structured organisations quite often don't spend enough time formalising how their salespeople work, what exactly they do while interacting with prospects and clients, or even what the buyers expect to experience while interacting with the salespeople.

They just tend to take for granted what the salespeople should be doing. Most probably they know how they work and what they are expected to do, especially sales directors, but if you ask them to write it down, they might trip. It is mainly a lack of formalisation, not a lack of know-how. Thus enquiring of them in a proper way enables us to unveil the sequence of actions that shape the interaction process with prospects, the journey each

---

* Attributed to Abraham Lincoln, on politics.
† Cialdini, R., *Influence: The Psychology of Persuasion*, Harper Business, 1984.

prospect generally takes from the stage of unawareness to the purchasing act, or just up to the point when the prospect decides to quit.

To structure it under a simple approach, we can divide the process into stages; at each stage, certain actions are expected and they should provide an output.

Stages are in sequence as ideally the journey will have a starting point -the entrance into the process-, then some steps to be performed before reaching an end where prospects will exit the process for better or for worse. Obviously, in a figurative journey people can jump stages getting different shortcuts, or take longer to get accustomed to the process. Designing the sales process means defining those stages in a way that depicts what is expected to be done in each of them and what outcome is expected.

Sales Process Stages

In many cases, the use of sales stages is merely a static naming convention, including, for instance, "Contact Made," "Proposal Sent," or "Negotiation." We argue that naming each stage in a more dynamic way exerts an effect on people who have to act accordingly. The idea is not to create a repository for deals and opportunities once "contact has been made," but to constantly remind to salespeople what is expected to be done. This technique applies a strong driver to what is to be done well beyond the simple silos of stages to be filled of contacts data, but more as a dynamic workflow that salespeople run by each single action. Actions that are well described in each stage naming.

For this reason, we list below a broader suggestion of stages' definitions to name them with the perspective of enabling efficiency in sales process management.

Lead-In

When entering the process cold, deals have to be processed starting with an "in" phase. When a new contact comes in touch with the brand, it should be passed to the salespeople's attention, enabling them to take care of that person. Often in this stage, a marketing automation tool pushes new contacts which have been dug out of the market using marketing techniques, and in this stage it is expected that salespeople would reach out and start working with them.

This stage can also be an assignment zone where salespeople are not yet involved; in this case, a process will create the allocation of each deal to the correct salesperson. Hence another stage can be in place—a stage in which getting in contact with the leads is the outcome. If the lead generation can produce that assignment, then the very first stage can be directly actionable, that is, Contacting.

Contacting

Here each salesperson can manage a list of new opportunities to start working on and then initiate them into the process. Actions to do are the list of activities the organisation planned for the contact procedure, either in voice or by messaging, largely depending on the specific market's pattern habits. The outcomes are the first understanding of the prospect and the verification of any opportunity in place. There is also an important difference between "cold leads," people who know nothing about our company/proposal, and people who have already expressed some interest in us. Cold leads imply "cold callings" as it uses lists of contacts bought or (legally) developed. For instance, an industry directory can provide hundreds or even thousands of phone numbers and email addresses, generally speaking company email addresses, or they can be found by scraping (more or less legally) social media like LinkedIn. The latter allows users to download lists with data when people have given permission for their contact data to be distributed, an occurrence that is becoming rare.

In a few words, any time a company starts its sales process using cold leads, salespeople face a challenge: get the attention of their counterpart via "out-of-the-blue" contact. This was a quite effective method in the earlier era of telemarketing; however, in today's market an excessive use of this approach has made it questionable.

When the list of new leads is created based on people who have already expressed interest in what we do, in our company's brand and value proposition, then salespeople can operate in a more comfortable way, not bothering "innocent" people who know nothing about them but getting in contact with market operators who are, at least, in search mode. Such new leads comprise people who are aware of the problem they need to solve and are actively looking for solutions. Hence they have already expressed interest in the brand/company and a contact from the company doesn't fall totally unattended. In the CRM jargon, they are called "Hot Leads."

What can happen when the process focuses on cold-leads nurture/development is that salespeople have to focus their abilities on engaging completely unknown people in a conversation. The purpose of the interaction is to nurture a need, raising awareness of the (possible) problem, in people who are often not prepared for it. If this is quite usual in some B2C business models, it is, unfortunately, also widely adopted in B2B markets too: the procedure of calling up a list of companies (within a sector) to dig out someone interested in a solution (for a specific problem), is widely known in the marketing industry as a common procedure of B2B lead generation.

When instead the lead contacting is operated on lists of leads who have, at least, expressed an interest in what we do/propose, then getting contacted is not totally unexpected. Thus the focus of those sales processes is more on the quality of the following part of the process: on providing them a valuable experience of the brand/company. This includes nurturing the counterpart's interest in the possible solution they are possibly actively looking for, to solve a problem they are aware of. Hence the skills of the salespeople become more relevant into the next stages of the process.

Also, the "Contacting" stage could be merged with the following one: "Discovering Opportunities." Nothing blocks salespeople from moving into that mode right away when they are just in the Contact mode. Our logical division in stages has the purpose of clarifying what has to be done and what has to be the outcome of certain activities. The Sales Process is not to be intended as a series of independent silos, but as part of an organic flow where actions have to be put in place at the right time by well-prepared sales personnel. The human touch is essential in this type of sales process. Otherwise we would refer to machine sales: an e-commerce, as an unmanned process that follows different rules under control of a designed CRM technology.

Discovering Opportunities

This stage can take place at the same time of "Contacting", or it can be moved to a time when meeting the counterpart will be fully dedicated to this analysis. This stage could also be the first one when a dedicated Contacting stage is not in place, like after the "Lead-In" stage. We believe in the importance of listing it separately to highlight the relevance of the Discovery Opportunities' outcome: understanding the requests and expectations of the (potential) customer. Discover, by asking what the prospect is looking for, is sometimes an activity that is truly undervalued.

Time pressure often makes salespeople (and even more so sales directors or entrepreneurs) keen to get a shortcut: assuming they have got what the client wants with a limited or even no discovery session at all. This is a very common mistake in sales: running ahead without a proper understanding of what the counterpart, the client, is really looking for taking assumptions.

The feeling is that personal productivity relies on the capability to run each task in the fastest possible way. Which, by all means, is also true. But when we work with other humans, the capability to be able to define the right velocity to move from A to B is complex and, in some way, something odd that largely depends on the counterpart we are working with. Thus, productivity in sales can be complex to assess and control. Complex but not impossible.

To reach that goal of productivity assessment and control, we strongly suggest putting in place the sales process stages in accordance with this method, not slavishly, but by applying the organisation's culture and employees' personal creativity.

By adding a dedicated stage, namely "Discovering Opportunities," the activities to perform become more clear: it is imperative to dig out every detail about the opportunity/opportunities, using a set of queries that enables a proper unveiling of the situation, of the expectations and about the counterpart's feelings.

The queries' methodology is nothing new,* but is still quite unknown. Experienced, well-trained salespeople are the ones who can apply the queries' methodology† with confidence. They are able to perform the art of questioning in such a smooth manner that it avoids leaving the recipient with a bad taste in their mouth: *"Are they putting me under probing questioning?"*

The querying process can be very warm and comfortable for prospects already keen to buy from you, while cold leads could be more reluctant to answer. If performed in the correct fashion the queries process is not only comfortable but also extremely powerful in motivating the prospect to stick with it and to the sales person. It has been proved‡ that salespeople who ask more questions, with the candid intention to understand and help the clients in getting the best for themselves, perform better in sales. Discovering

---

* Barber, J., *Good Question! The Art of Asking Questions to Bring a Positive Change*, Book Shaker, 2005.
† Fisher, R., Ury, W., *Getting to Yes: Negotiating an Agreement without Giving In*, Random House, 2012.
‡ Grant, A., *Give and Take*, Penguin Books, 2014.

Opportunities is then an extremely important stage, where not only each sales person is enabled to better understand what the client really needs, but even more importantly because it is a process capable of pushing the relationship to a new level, becoming more meaningful and resourceful. Trust is a matter of intentions, hence being able to truly act with the best intentions is a powerful driving force that people perceive, a force that leads to winning trust, a force that enables better selling.

Discovery Opportunities is, then, a powerful sales tool and not just a stage along a process. Due to its power it should be performed during every sales process, no matter what, if we want to enhance the success rate.

Qualification

As per the previous stage, Qualification can also be conducted earlier, at the time of the very first contact. We believe that the sequence should be followed as presented: first Discovering Opportunities and then Qualification, not the other way around.

Moreover, keeping the two quests separate as concepts and behaviours allows us to perform a better qualification of the person first and foremost in order to engage that person before investing effort to explain what we can do for our counterpart.

Comprehending the problem and the expected solution is paramount, only then we would proceed further: if the person/organisation really matches the parameters to bring us effective and successful business.

Here is where this method enables the greatest benefit: by not mixing the two analyses together and avoiding easy leaps into discussing what we can do for the client.

Businesses should know who their ideal clients are, then they need to be able to select them among the many potential opportunities: with a process that outlines when a prospect fits into the parameters for being a (good) client.

On this duty sits one of the most important sales issues, an entanglement that also implies how salespeople should work, how they should be compensated and what are the expected outcomes.

It is often debated whether businesses should say "NO" to clients; no matter if you are a solopreneur, a professional or a multimillion company, some clients are better to let go. But while it is important to be aware of problems that can arise by engaging wrong clients, no business can in fact really feel good about the action of saying "NO" to clients hence to get rid of opportunities.

It is considered that opportunities are scattered to anyone in business. Thus, it is neither in the business people's way of life nor in the salespeople's mandate to tell a prospect: *"We do not want you."*

What can, instead, be effectively done is to clarify the conditions under which any opportunity has to fall, thus making the counterparts accountable for matching those conditions. The ability to be clear upon what is relevant, the conditions, will allow people in sales to provide an honest framework for the service production. Hence filtering opportunities with fine mesh filters to move forward only with the ones that match the conditions is the final purpose of this stage.

More than merely a matter of saying "NO," it is a matter of engaging the counterpart to show and declare a positive intention to fit into those rules in order to obtain the solution that solves her or his problem.

Cialdini explained extremely well the way in which, by adopting the law of scarcity, salespeople can make their client feel eager to win the game, and getting in possession of the (scarce) product they were, earlier, just curious about.*

The qualification process can have a similar effect on the prospects who approach a possible solution they are interested in. The reason is TIME.

It has often been said that B2C marketing and sales techniques are different from the rules in B2B markets. Hence the sales techniques often used to mislead, manipulate or just persuade a single person, the consumer, don't work when the buyer is an organisation. In general terms, this is true, but we should check specifically how some methods or techniques can actually bear results.

Considering the law of scarcity, leveraging it can actually work during a sales process with a professional counterpart under some circumstances:

■ The object of the contract is complex solutions or products with a limited number of possible suppliers.
■ The product or service is effectively mission-critical for the client.
■ The time frame for the solution to be in place is limited, better if it is really short.

---

* Cialdini, R., ibidem.

Business buyers also are people, and even if some of them, the professional buyers, can play the game with the same or even better weapons than average salespeople, under the previous circumstances also them can feel the pressure of time, the need to rely on a trustworthy provider, the need to procure something that wouldn't be extremely easy to find elsewhere and which is relevant for their own business to survive.

To be clear, the range of solutions that fall into this framework is not as trivial as many of us can be tempted to think. And, in many ways, the businesses that have been able to leverage those factors are the ones that thrive. Being able to recognise when one or all of those conditions are in place then leverage them is what a well-designed sales process should enable in the sales person.

Discovering Opportunities and Qualification stages are designed to enable salespeople to perform those checks and collect information and data that can depict the client's condition so that the proposing solution can benefit from that very knowledge.

If this rule is considered less relevant for sales of products than sales of services, it is because products are often ready to ship while services imply a co-production stage or at least a greater involvement of the client.* But when products also include an amount of service, then a more detailed analysis of the clientele can help to avoid or reduce following problems and possible related shrinkage of the economic return of the business.

Qualifying the opportunities in the most efficient way is, then, one of the most important stages of the sales process, and it is a duty of the organisation culture to make sure of how this stage is properly set in place, and also how salespeople should manage the filtering: the more strict the filter is, the fewer opportunities will move forward. Tightening the filter will affect the output of the whole sales process that will hit a lower level of turnover. The greatest problem arises when salespeople are rewarded just on the turnover. A reward system is a powerful driver of people's behaviours; the structure of the reward directs the way in which people work, what they believe in and the values they nurture in their daily commitment.

When the reward system focuses just on the total amount of money resulting from the sales process (turnover), it gives salespeople the message that it is not important who the client is or what he or she needs, while the only important matter is how much the deal is worth. This approach can't

---

* Carlzon, J., *Moments of Truth*, Ballinger Pub Co., 1987.

encourage people to use the proper filtering procedure: anything that boosts turnover will be OK under this framework.

In the opposite situation, salespeople who have no adequate incentives, neither on turnover nor in qualitative deals, could be less keen to move deals ahead if they are even suspected of bringing in any problem. Under this framework, they can use an ultra-fine mesh filter in pursuit of peace of mind for themselves and for the organisation.

The qualification stage plays a fundamental role in the business's health, by letting only selected, suitable deals pass through, it enables the business to reduce risk and losses. On the other hand, the purpose of the sales process is to bring in the maximum amount of new business (in accordance with the business plans and capabilities). We can therefore see the qualification stage as probably the central duty that gives sales their direction: growing the business via good, appropriate deals and suitable clients.

In operative words, the qualification stage should be performed by engaging the clients with clear purposes, delivering clear messages on what is important to share to help them successfully.

The Discovering Opportunities is a kind of "*let's now understand what exactly you need and if we can make it for you...*" enquiry, (a method that places on the client the effort to bring the sales person on board on the solution requested). The qualification stage would instead be a sort of "*Ok, now let's understand if you match the criteria to be a good client.*"

Allow us a bit of drama: please don't try to use the second statement verbatim if you are not a close friend of the client!

The focus should be on the intention behind it; when queries are used in the proper way, this method is assessed to be extremely powerful and persuasive in engaging the client in the deal (scarcity law).*

Hence keeping the stages "Developing Opportunities" and "Qualification" well defined, enclosed and separated is a way to give them importance, structure and gravity. Even if along the way experienced salespeople can mix them, adapting them to the flow of the single, unique relationship and interaction they develop with each client.

Qualification Methods

In order to support the salespeople in their process to assess each client/deal, there are some effective frameworks that, likewise the 4Ps marketing mix for

---

* Cialdini, R., ibidem.

marketers, help to guide the action of salespeople when they are about to check the matching of qualification parameters. Just like a list of checks to keep in mind and tick one by one, the model BANT is the 4-digit model of client qualification, while the MEDDIC is the more extended 6-digit model.

BANT is the acronym for:

■ Budget
■ Authority
■ Needs
■ Time

To clarify it, let's go through each part.

BANT explained

Budget

This comes first mainly to make the acronym work but also because without an available budget we all risk spending time for nothing.

It is always tricky to ask a client: *"Can you pay for it?"* But it is even more tricky to assume arbitrarily that he or she will be keen to pay the right amount. For sure enquiring about availability to pay can leave a bad taste in the client's mouth, so the salesperson should find a way to ask that not only in a manner that avoids hurting the client but also leverages the law of scarcity to engage the client's commitment in the deal.*

The way to pursue the real answer requires patience, empathy and language control. Take it slow: do not ask it as the very first question, engage in discussing the solution the client really needs, reinforce the counterpart's eagerness in getting exactly the solution you are talking about. Reinforce the focus on the benefit the client is pursuing by adopting that product/solution. Then the client will be more open to evaluating the effort he or she is ready to face.

Quite often the available budget enquiry comes last in the process; even if it may be a yes/no condition, making it last can sweeten the pill. The more the client perceives it as a collaborative, well-intended request for information, aimed to co-create the solution that fits the client's

---

* Cialdini, R., ibidem.

requirements, the more the client will be open to unveiling it. It is probably the most important point of the four, and that's why it should be performed last!

One more thing: you shouldn't believe you have to stay within the client's budget.

The budget is merely one dimension of the compensation the client is available to pay in order to get what was a very initial idea of a possible solution; while any added value can change that intention. Hence we now come back to the relevance of the "Discovering Opportunities" stage: if that quest was properly run we can now match the information. The outcome of the two pieces of information joined will be the understanding of the client's awareness about the complexity of the solution previously figured, and whether, how much he or she is prepared to pay for it.

If the outcome is not positive, then the sales person has the option to try to bridge the gap between expectations and the intent to pay. That bridging can rely on lowering the client's expectations about the solution requested (reducing its cost) or (better) raising the client's perception of the intrinsic value. Hence having appropriately performed the Discovering Opportunities quest before, will enable the salesperson to manage the situation for a better outcome.

Authority

What if we invest time in convincing the counterpart only to discover too late that the person we convinced is not the decision-maker? It is not only a matter of time, which is also important, but anyone who has tested what it means to start the process again knows that the second process will never be the same. If we achieved a positive outcome with the first person, there is a risk that we wouldn't get the same with the second one!

Jokes aside (half serious), if the person we are talking to is not the decision-maker, it is better to know it as soon as possible. The process itself needs to be changed if the counterpart is not the buyer but a user or just a stakeholder. The content to share may not be the same, the persuasion levers might be different, and thus the process might leverage other pillars according to the role of the two different persons. The main risk of this title void is to take for granted the requiring person as the buyer, responsible for decision-making. It can lead to mistakes and an excess of effort addressed to the wrong person.

Efficiency is also about making the right things, not just making things right.

Needs

Salespeople may tend to avoid this point in the mistaken belief that it is enough to talk about what the client wants or about the product/solution we are going to offer, so the doubt is: *"Why should I ask again what he or she needs?"*

But this title is not about the explicit requirements the client expressed (or would have expressed) at the Discovering Opportunities stage. Not at all. Here we have the opportunity to enquire about the person we are talking to, that person who owns an agenda. An experienced sales person knows how important it is to know what her/his main goals are, what he or she expects from this process, what are the benefits, opportunities and possible outcomes.

Also, in B2B most of the time we talk to people and those persons have needs and expectations we have to understand. Giving answers directly to those personal expectations and queries matter for the deal's success more than most salespeople tend to believe.

In Hitch,* a great Will Smith film, Alex "Hitch" Hitchens meets a prospect who candidly confesses his unethical intentions about the girl he wants to win.

Hitch reacts quite badly to it, not only refusing to take the deal on board but threatening the guy if he wouldn't let him go.

Without reacting like Hitch, being aware of the personal intention behind the buyer's involvement in the purchasing process is relevant for the sales person. We can't argue about the ethical inner drivers of each business and how they direct the behaviour in sales. More often it is not about going beyond the ethics of business, but about understanding what drives our human counterparts.

But let's stay on the value of the information for the sales process:

■ First, it gives a clearer picture of how to fill in the personal expectations of our counterpart, who ultimately is the decision-maker (Authority).

---

* Tennant, A., *Hitch-The Cure for Common Men*, Columbia Picts, 2005.

■ Second, it gives the seller more tools to leverage when they come to objections and value negotiation.

What we shouldn't deny is that in certain cases personal drivers can be stronger than the logical and analytical ranking of the purchase's pros and cons.*

Time

Time is often the most valuable tool of a seller. As time is simultaneously the most valuable asset and the most scarce, being able to engage with the time perception and time-fit requirements of the client is an invaluable ability to manage any sales process. Hence assessing the time expectations of the client is essential, as many salespeople know that, upon this lies the potential deal.

■ First, a proper enquiry about the client's request can unveil much about the counterpart. It reveals a lot about their own perception, knowledge and awareness of the purchasing process and the solution's creation time.
■ Second, it says a lot about how urgently the solution is needed.

When the client's request is not compatible with the purchasing process or the solution's availability, the sales person might learn something important here. Enquiring more the client to unveil the game further can highlight some main scenarios:

1. Lack of awareness and/or overconfidence on the possibility to procure the solution faster than (considered) possible.
2. The client relies on information from other providers who alternatively
   a. voluntarily misled him; or
   b. have the solution ready to ship; or
   c. rely on a faster production process.
3. The client's urgency to procure the solution shows
   a. the client urgently needs the solution; or
   b. the client has started the purchasing process in time.

---

* Cialdini, R., ibidem.

Let's try to guess some scenarios upon the previous data matching:

The client has started the process in time and has allocated a proper time frame to procure the solution.

- Making enquiries will support the client's confidence in their perception that the salesperson is collecting information to provide the best service.
- Then proceeding with quality along the sales process can be vital. The client can be well organised and prepared to deal with the business properly and can expect a similar approach from suppliers. Salespeople should try to engage the client on the very same register, avoiding shortcuts or simplification.

The client declares a short time for the procurement process.

- The sales person has to enquire carefully about the client's reasons, as the perception acquired from enquiring could clash with the sense of urgency of the counterpart, but it is essential for the seller to learn:
  - what information the client has;
  - what he or she really knows about the solution; and
  - why the client needs the solution so urgently.
- The counterpart could be less sensitive to the quality of the process. Sellers should test it, evaluating carefully what drives the client. If they have wrong information, correcting them can be extremely difficult. Sometimes a proper assessment of the information and a demonstration of the true reasons can take the salesperson to a higher position, from where he or she can leverage the credibility gained. This happens more frequently when the solution is really mission-critical. If the critical mission is not in place or not already perceived, then the sales person has the hard job of testing whether there is room to educate the counterpart or deciding to dismiss the deal as unqualified.

The time is achievable even if it is compact.

- The information is invaluable as it allows the salesperson to leverage the value of the solution using the time/price dichotomy.
- The client has the power to change their expectations, hence investing time to support the client's decision by providing an informative service can enable both parties to win trust and to get closer to winning the deal. That is to say, just get closer, not win it yet.

Time can be considered the check of the qualification stage: working on it enables salespeople to perform better in their sales processes management and, ultimately, convert more opportunities. The real trouble is that it can require a lot of time.

MEDDIC/MEDDICC

This qualification method* is attributed to Dick Dunkel, John McMahon and Jack Napoli who developed it together as sales trainers in PTC, in 1996.

In fact this is an extended version of the BANT acronym, which allows salespeople to keep under control some more parameters pertaining to the same purpose: understanding if the deal can be qualified. It also introduces a slightly different perspective on the way to analyse elements; it can help when the organisation's culture prefers this approach.

■ Metrics: Identifying key parameters that justify the economic exchange
■ Economic buyer: Who the decision-maker is
■ Decision process: How the purchasing process works and is run
■ Decision criteria: Analysis of the main criteria that affect the decision
■ Identify pain: The problem in place, what the client needs to achieve, the problem/solution approach
■ Champion: Stakeholders' control of and influence on the decision

And eventually

■ Competition: Analysis of the competitive landscape to be aware of the client's options

There is no need to go through each item, as it wouldn't help much in clarifying the purpose of the Qualification stage. We just notice whether the model actually embeds the Discovering Solutions stage in the metrics, such as identifying pain, decision criteria, decision process and competition, and introduces some complexity such as stakeholders' influence, that is correct to point it out. The benefit of this model is to recall more elements in one place, while the limitation is its reduced simplicity. On the other hand, the BANT model's benefit is its simplicity and direct actionable tasks, while its

---

* White, A., *MEDDICC: The Ultimate Guide to Stay One Step Ahead in the Complex Sale*, Meddicc Ltd, 2020.

limitations pertain to the modelisation and excessive simplification of a complex process. This is something that MEDDICC model does not resolve as, even more, it includes tasks that, in several authors' opinion, would require an adequate clear space* to be performed properly.

When in 1964 Neil Borden developed the 4Ps model the world applauded it; the great benefit of simplification helped masses of salespeople and entrepreneurs to understand what marketing was.†

Some years later Booms and Bitner proposed to raise those Ps to 7.‡ But credited to Philipp Kotler a motto started to circulate: *"No matter how many Ps you list, there is only one P that matters: People."* Whether the author is right or not, it shows that reduction of complexity is always in place to help, "as things should be made as simple as possible, but not simpler".§

Qualification Purpose and Outcome

As mentioned previously, the purpose of this stage is to clear the crowd of opportunities to focus the organisation's resources on the best ones. Even if many businesses tend to show excessive appetite when it comes to sales, and their internal culture implies that *"...no deal or client exists that shouldn't be dealt with."* The appraisal of opportunities should still be run if for no other reason than to ensure a better negotiation. Organisations who imagine they can serve everyone, run often less successful businesses; in their sales processes, the loss of an opportunity which is very often a client's decision is frequently considered a salesperson's failure.

We can notice a positive correlation between the success of an organisation and its ability to serve certain customers but not all of them. Sometimes organisations are able to create a market upon that knowledge: a need not yet fulfilled of a niche of clients can be their best market.

Developing Solutions

Here the focus is on depicting or designing the solution. This is what salespeople generally enjoy the most. Very often confident salespersons who

---

* Grant, A., ibidem; Cialdini, R., ibidem.
† Borden, N., *The Concept of the Marketing Mix*, Wiley, 1964.
‡ Booms, B., Bitner, M. J., *Marketing Strategies and Organizational Structures for Service Firms*, in James H. Donnelly and William R. George, (eds), *Marketing of Services*, American Marketing Association, 1981.
§ Credited to Albert Einstein.

are in love with their job and tend to apply their real passion much more than an effective, deep strategic analysis, in order to achieve sales performance can use well-developed oratorical skills in talking about the object of the proposal, either a service or a product, with a swinging enthusiasm aimed at engaging their counterpart. Sales pitching is such an important skill when it is well-rooted in a strong and well-designed sales process, but it is greatly overrated when it is the lone skill leveraged by a salesperson who only relies on it to succeed. That mistake of skill's value has fostered a sort of human reaction which has reached the point of depicting salespeople as not pleasant to be around.* And entrepreneurs who love their products, who are product-people, oriented to the best product quality,† are the first to fall in love with that style. Then of course clients also fall in love with such an amazing way to engage interest. There is only one minor issue: the clients who fall in love are the ones who are *in line* with the proposed solution/product. They are the ones who were seeking it, hence they love when someone can explain it with an enthusiasm that draws them into every benefit of the service/product. Every other person, not really engaged yet in the proposed solution, will just be annoyed by that and more often than not they will lose interest completely.

Why does that happen? Is it not the main skill of a salesperson to sell the product/service for the best?

It does happen because the function of *sales* is often misunderstood. In certain cultures, *sales* means convincing someone with: *"Look how good my product is!"* Something that was true when the market was crowded of buyers and sellers led the game (unbelievably it happened not too long ago). At that time it was enough to be good at explaining the product/service to be successful in sales.

Hence the common belief that a good salesperson is someone who can convince others about his product. But sales dynamics have dramatically changed since the market changed, something that became evident at the turn of the century.

Nowadays sales can be really complex and require a methodology more than improvisation and, according to the kind of business and market, they also require a pattern of skills much more complete than just talking well.

---

* Credited to Woody Allen: *"There are worse things in life than death. Have you ever spent an evening with an insurance salesman?"*.
† Sirolli, E., *Trinity of Management*, Sirolli Institute, 2012.

We do not diminish the value of the ability to engage the client with storytelling and convince them with rhetoric when it is time to engage them with the solution. Nevertheless, we have to highlight the importance of all the other skills and tasks of the sales process and the necessary ability to balance and play with all of them. It is true that a great actor who engages audiences with great rhetorical art can be amazing to see, but what if the piece was badly written?

In the same way, it can be very sad to assist a great performance about the solution under proposal done by an enthusiastic salesperson who arrived at it after having made a series of wrong assumptions.

Hence the Developing Solutions stage is much more than just explaining it.

Of course, the simpler the solution is, the easier this stage will be. If it is clear that the client is there to buy a Ferrari, it is also very easy to assume what he or she would like to hear. Even if selling a Ferrari is not always as easy as pie; if we assume the solution is something easy and clear, jumping to explain it would seem the faster and better way to win the client with a reduced effort.

This will become much more evident when we discuss complex solutions that imply several options and how they can dramatically affect the experience, the value or the price. As well as many other aspects in the client's perception.

The idea of Developing Solutions comes from the technique used by complex solution salespeople who take the client with them and go through the solution design, the shaping of it—as much as it can be done according to the business/market—and truly assess a pattern of choices and features by querying the client. It is actually a real process to develop the final version of the solution tailored to the client.

In every industry where solutions are developed for the client, the procedure is well known, but sometimes even for much simpler products or services there are many custom options which allow a walking-through process that makes the client an active part of shaping the solution to fit their needs.

BTW, can you imagine a Ferrari buyer who doesn't ask for anything more than a standard basic model?

The Developing Solutions stage is gaining importance in a growing number of markets and businesses as options and customisation become a competition battlefield.

In terms of the walking-through process, we can consider some areas where the seller can lead the client. Let's try to list the most relevant of them in two groups—products and services—with the purpose of highlighting what can be considered most relevant for each of them.

Product

The subject of products can be covered under five main topics:

1. Features
2. User's value
3. Benefits
4. Value added
5. Competitor comparison

When shaping a product, it is extremely easy to discuss any feature to add. Depending on the client's perception of needs, the seller can explain each possible feature and its added value to the product as this can support the client's decision-making process.

The user's perceived value of a product largely depends on the user's purpose related to the product itself.

Benefits can be extras to add on top of the user's value of the product.

The salesperson can properly highlight them to make the counterpart aware of them. Extra benefits are unexpected and can be perceived as free value added to the product use.

The value added is mainly related to the client's purpose of use. Knowing what product is going to be substituted and what the choices are, the salesperson can leverage the client's perception of the value of use, and, even more, leverage how this solution could add any extra value in its use.

Comparison with competitors can be tricky. Experienced salespeople rarely go there, to avoid leaving the impression that they are just diminishing others' products in order to make theirs look better. But notwithstanding that, sometimes helping the client to compare products can be useful; avoid forcing any point of view or opinion, but use facts-based analysis and the process of enquiring about what the client needs and how this or the other product will fit into that pattern of needs.

This can be a very hard task for any seller who is keen to use shortcuts, or who tends to be overconfident about the product he or she is selling, having limited awareness of the competitive landscape. Compare other solutions, to work successfully, requires a truly open mind, a deep knowledge of most—if not all—of the solutions that can compete, and an effective client-centred approach based on the intention to truly achieve the best for the client (well beyond our own need to sell).

This is the reason why organisational culture matters so much with regard to this task performance: when the company has a customer-centric culture, it enables each salesperson to develop this approach and be the client's ally in the product selection.

Service

Service can be covered under three main topics:

1. User's experience
2. User's value
3. Outcome

Services have the characteristic that they do not exist until they are created with the client.* Hence they differ from products as during the service's sales process the object doesn't exist and the value perception largely depends on the user's experience of the service co-creation. In some way this is also a relevant part of the product's value, likewise the user experience of a physical object really matters to the user's perception of value and it is considered, nowadays, the ultimate competitive battlefield. But for services this subject becomes of paramount importance.

> *An amazing Alan Arkin partnering with a wonderful Michael Douglas in The Kominsky Method (Netflix, 2018), comments on the water pressure of the hotel shower where they are spending one night: "I'd love to pay more for a hotel with proper water pressure"*

The value of the service itself clearly depends on the user's purpose, but how to leverage this is what matters the most. Salespeople should have a clear plan of what actions affect the counterpart's perception of value, matching the user's purposes to the offered service features. Salespeople who only rely on the brand's image and do not feel any need to engage the clientele on what they will get from the service developed under that very brand are not using the opportunity for leverage to boost the user's experience during the sales process!

---

* Carlzon, J., *Moments of Truth*, Ballinger Pub Co., 1987.

Experienced salespeople know that a service always implies a larger outcome than merely its individual service purpose. The complex task of transferring to the counterpart an appropriate awareness of "all possible" outcomes the client will be able to achieve via the specific service, will influence the client's value perception. Hence this capability of a salesperson is absolutely necessary and relevant for the sales process success. This could also be a new and enhanced use of the salesperson's oratorical ability to engage the client in foreseeing the solution's qualities.

Therefore, Developing Solutions is the stage where salespeople can unleash their historically attributed disposition to leverage people's emotions to engage their counterparts' feelings and persuade them. It is not really important whether the deal regards products or services, even though some specificity of the two can suggest a fine-tuning of the process. The Developing Solutions stage is where salespeople engage the prospective client exploiting their best skill in the art of persuasion* by using storytelling, rhetorical methods and empathy with the person before them. But what is extremely important is to clarify that all those qualities can be ineffective or even have a boomerang effect against the salesperson if not preceded by a diligent analysis that only comes from the Discovery Opportunities and Qualification stages.

To sum it up, we can say that the whole process up to this point, if rigorously applied, is a construction of the last stage: the Negotiation. To be precise, a successful, modern sales process consists of three phases:

1. Analysis
2. Exploitation
3. Negotiation

First comes deep analysis of the client, starting from any explicit requirement to concealed and untold personal expectations and needs. When properly run, the analysis can unveil powerful information that the salesperson can exploit during the discussion to engage the client with the solution.

The analysis phase, which takes place either in the Discovery Opportunities or the Qualification stages, supports the Developing Solutions phase. In this view the Developing Solutions phase represents the outcome of the analysis, and it should rely on a client-centric approach operated by the competence of asking questions.

---

* Cialdini, R., ibidem.

The Art of Asking Questions,* which boosts empathy, nurtures a reciprocal understanding and engages the counterpart in the co-creation from the early stage of interaction, thus enabling the highest success rate in sales.†
Most successful sales processes are developed with that customer-centric approach, as they are based on good intentions and salespeople have been well educated in mastering the art of questioning.‡

Those phases of analysis and exploitation together have the purpose of engaging prospective clients in the solution shaping, hence giving them the clearest idea of how the solution truly matches their needs.

The expected outcome of the first part of the sales process is a situation where a potential client is much keener to conclude the deal with the salesperson who led the process; thus, the client has a better understanding of the value of the deal and is aware of the conditions under which he or she can procure that product/service.

In a few words, someone who is eager to close the deal.

This will introduce us to the next and final stage of the sales process: Negotiation.

Negotiation

If it gets to this stage, a deal has a good chance of being won. Theoretically, if all the previous steps of the process have been led with accuracy and tasks have been consciously deployed—and there has also been included quite a touch of luck—then closing the deal should be just a matter of deciding its ancillary conditions.

In fact more often than not negotiation is not an easy piece of work; but quite the opposite. When it comes to actually putting the signature on the bottom line, very often major complexities arise.

The theory is that there shouldn't be any difficulty if the preceding process has been developed meticulously; thus an agreement would be possible and only requires some more understanding from both sides. Making a step forward from both the seller's and the buyer's side is possible as there is an area where both parties have the very same intention to be in accord. It implies that when this doesn't happen, a problem can be found in the

---

* Fadem, T. J., *The Art of Asking: Ask Better Questions, Get Better Answers*, Pearson Education, 2009.
† Cherry, P., *Questions that Sell: The Powerful Process for Discovering What Your Customer Wants*, Amacom, 2018.
‡ Gee, V., Gee, J., *OPEN-Question Selling: Unlock Your Customer's Needs to Close the Sale... By Knowing What to Ask and When to Ask*, McGraw Hill, 2007.

process—maybe something hasn't been performed properly, or some data have not been taken into account at the right time, or maybe even someone has misled the counterpart (which is not always just the salesperson).

If it is quite logical and straightforward to agree that a properly developed process should enable a smooth negotiation, it can be not so clear how to relate the missing agreement problem with any previous issue or even less how to connect the difficulties in getting a "yes" from the counterpart with some earlier visible mistake or misunderstanding.*

Many books are available on negotiation, and the complexity of it is suggested by the existence of professional negotiators. Organisations require the engagement of these professionals when strong negotiation skills are needed to develop complex, multiple-side agreements upon critical issues.

We do not want to explain how to negotiate or how a proper negotiation should appear; in this book, we only have the opportunity to clarify how the sales process works systematically and how each part of it has an effect somewhere else.

If we are not aware of the system dynamics in the sales process, then it becomes possible that we will not be able to manage it for the best: even though the negotiation would go well most of the time, we could be far from the optimal point without being aware of it.

When trying to figure out some connections between visible effects in the negotiation stage and their roots in the sales process, we can answer by defining what people should or shouldn't do in each stage/situation. But this would be a prescriptive approach which is not the intention of this book, we only aim to give readers food for thought and enable you all in getting confident in developing your own vision of the ideal sales process for your business. Especially now that we are at the bottom of the sales process management topic discussion, and having described each stage in detail, we can be pretty sure most readers have got the sense of what we tried to explain, and they are already empowered by a complete framework of ideas, perhaps not new ones, but better formalised and indexed.

Hence, we just highlight how connections work with the intention of clarifying a way to operate the analysis when any sales director, entrepreneur or business person will be looking for wiring back problems of the sales process with possible roots along the process itself.

---

* Fisher, R., Ury, W., *Getting into Yes. Negotiating an Agreement without Giving In*, Random House, 2012.

Difficulties at the negotiation stage are generally related to the client's experience along the process. One common case might happen when the enquiring process suffers a misunderstanding or fails to bring empathy to the interaction. When we, as clients, feel uncomfortable under probing questioning from a salesperson that seems to have no reason, we can issue our rebuke at any time—such as later, during negotiations—according to our own, unexpressed purposes.

When sellers are in the process of querying their counterparts they should be trained to master the Art of Making Questions in a way that creates the best experience for their counterparts and avoids rebuke.

Lack of analysis always brings problems during the Developing Solutions stage and any alteration or adjustment on the way to the solution already depicted can leave the client not fully convinced about the capability to understand what is expected by the whole provider company, not just the single salesperson.

Failure to foster engagement in the Developing Solutions stage can lead to troubles during negotiation as the client is not satisfied with the experience yet.

Working back this way by formulating questions about how the system works and how it should actually work, is the way to fix almost any problem in sales.

Learning Opportunity

The analysis of the sales process should, according to the preceding discussion, start from its outputs, understanding why prospects convert or quit (and when) and what they say or hide about the relationship with the brand.

Going back to each moment of truth* and wondering about them in order to know what a proper investigation can enable an efficiency improvement process is the course to be taken here. Because whether deals are lost or won, they all are, and should be, learning opportunities. Whether an organisation is about to redesign the sales process or just in pursuit of improvement, the analysis of the output is valuable when comprehending both, won and lost opportunities, and alongside the art of asking questions: strategic

---

* Gronroos, C., Gummesson, E. (Eds), *Service Marketing - Nordic School Perspectives*, Stockholm University, Stockholm, Research Report 1985, p. 2. Carlzon, J., (1987). *Moments of truth*, Cambridge, Mass. Ballinger.

questions that boost the search for the object, not aimed to find someone responsible for the wrongdoing.

Purpose and Outcome

We believe in designing the sales process by stages and dedicate a time slot to each of them; keeping the focus on each stage one at a time; reducing the possibility of mixing up procedures and keeping the quest practice clear. As we discussed before, experienced salespeople can actually mix everything up and play it for the best with every counterpart in a unique, dedicated performance. But, in pursuit of feeling confident and improvising, a good piece of advice is to master the rules first.* The purpose of planning, then running a sales process as designed, is to pursue a repetitive, measurable method that can be reviewed and improved by measurable changes.

The outcome of the process is to select the greatest number of prospects/ opportunities that only match the capability of the company on the production of those services/products: opportunities that can create more added value.

This really works well in theory. Thus, theoretical approaches are the ones that help to understand what could be done in real life; adopting high-level standards in organisations helps in the worse to fail to smaller, but acceptable results, than just setting low standards or not setting them at all.

Companies in pursuit of winning competitive advantages can leverage the continuous improvement of their sales processes, while the cost-effectiveness rate makes clear how the sales process output should be kept maximised for the sake of economic efficiency. This is why managing by plan and controlling the sales process matters for the whole business survivance.

Now readers have become aware of what to do to design their own businesses' sales process. Going through each stage depicted earlier, adapt them to the way each business should really sell, enabling it to match their prospect's expectations. Also, and foremost in terms of experience with the brands, when building their relationship with you, clients have expectations and biases that come from previous experience and knowledge. Being able to master the sales process enables everyone to use any CRM tool to design it and create every control and facilitation that enable each salesperson to stay with the planned fashion of sale.

---

* Attributed to Pablo Picasso: *"Learn the rules like a pro, so you can break them like an artist"*.

The CRM that you use as a tool is the digital extension, or a mirror, of the sales process, enabling everyone in the organisation to embed the organisation's culture, and it is worth mentioning:

We refer to complex sales processes related to mission-critical service or at least Specialties. For conveniences or not-relevant purchases, the process is often cut to a fraction of what we describe here.

Summary

The Sales Process is extremely relevant in B2B businesses where solutions or services are the object of the transaction, but it is also very true for products of relevant value or mission-critical purposes. In this chapter we went through the complexity of the Sales Process, and we showed how, in order to manage it for the best, organisations must carefully design it.

- It is important to clarify that CRM can make the difference between a modern, efficient and fluent management and a confused one.
- The Sales Process design implies stages and activities to be performed by people in sales.
- Each stage implies a dynamic process to achieve some milestones and tasks to do with and for the client.
- Creating a relationship with clients requires a structured, well-conducted series of actions that, like a dance, engage the counterpart in collaborating.
- Probably the most important activity to be performed in the Sales Process is the Qualification, a process of reciprocal understanding that not only provides to unveil if the opportunity fits to the organisation, but also engages the client in the deal creation.
- The job of sales dramatically changed in the last 10-15 years and modern salespeople rely on a pattern of skills well beyond the eloquence and manipulative art of persuasion.

The role of a CRM tool in sales is to support, guide and measure salespeople's daily effort in the management of deals and people behind them. The logic of the CRM as a marketing strategy is to enable the organisation in its mission in the market; planning the use of the digital tool very often implies the organisation to rethink its way to sell, define and declare how its policies can fit into the strategy, create a guidance and a behaviour control not to punish, but to learn and improve.

No other methods have been able to make it happen as much as a digital CRM tool implementation can nowadays. Organisations have an opportunity to grab to stay up to date with the unrested environment.

Chapter 4

Leads Generation

Streaming new fresh prospects into the sales process is what every business wants, it is vital to nurture client bases to keep businesses afloat. This
function is also part of the purpose of creating, developing and nurturing
relationships with clients even if, technically, it is not part of the CRM as a
tool. Leads generation is about operational marketing: engaging people with
content to attract interest and becoming visible by nurturing brand awareness. It foster interacting with interested people to pursue sales.

The topics covered in this chapter are as follows:

1. Leads, prospects and opportunities: Marketing
2. What engages people
3. What is Leads Generation
4. The buyer persona
5. Prospects and opportunities
6. From leads generation to CRM

Leads, Prospects and Opportunities: Marketing

Everyone is talking about leads generation; in the last few years, it has
become the mantra for business development. An automated system that
is able to create new fresh leads to whom to start selling is now the holy
grail that everyone needs to make their business thrive. Has anything been
recently discovered or developed by new technology or is lead generation
just a new name for something already in place?

DOI: 10.4324/9781003148388-4

New technology available for the generation of leads is not really about "what" engages people, but how it is possible to make it easier. Thus, marketing automations are powerful tools that enable marketers to save time on repetitive tasks, which means boosting everyone's productivity. While social media (would) enable reaching target audiences faster and more effectively.

In reality, social media have become powerful new ponds from where to fish out potentially interested people; for quite a long time, it has been easy to pull out leads using the great new features of digital media. Since the early stages of the social media era, businesses have relocated their marketing budgets to those channels getting remarkable ROI. However, leads generation performed by marketing automation as the solution to the business problem of engaging more people is not wholly correct. We know that shortcuts are attractive, while complex solutions are not so easy. Hence, referring to leads generation is more catchy than just saying "marketing," as we used to. It is true that marketing can have a wider meaning, while leads generation focuses on something more specific, but the result of this shortcut can be that the relevant role of a wider and more comprehensive approach over many aspects, which is the kernel of marketing, can get lost.

We suggest that the focus on the leads generation stage makes sense when a broader methodology of marketing is in place. While imagining that someone can just drop a hook in the pond to fish new clients would lead to mistakes, doing that after having nurtured the right stretch of water, as the final gesture of a well-prepared catch, is the recipe for success.

Marketing may have become a worn-out expression, but it is still the logic behind the business; let's talk about how to do better marketing then, and how to connect people, define prospects and finally build opportunities.

What Engages People

Leads are people, not objects -people who have preferences, thoughts and necessities-. We believe that taking shortcuts implies risk that does not value that concept enough. People engagement relies on the capability to give them a value, something relevant for them, something they would even be prepared to pay for. The relationship with audiences matters, regardless of whether we have something remarkable to say or not. In those two options it is only the outcome that differs.

The point of marketing is to catch people's attention and to get them interested in your product. However, so much of marketing consists of regular old brown cows; the ads (and the products) all look the same. They're not remarkable enough to pull people away from their busy lives and trusted products or services. That's why you need a Purple Cow: something truly remarkable that will catch people's interest."

This is how Seth Godin was intending to be "remarkable" in his 2005 book, something unexpected, out of the ordinary. And it was a remarkable book indeed!

I'm sure we all can distinguish between something remarkable, which is out of ordinary but valuable, against something else which is just out of ordinary. Well, ok, maybe not really everyone can do that... Ok, let's skip that.

Remarkable is something that is valuable and presented in a way that grabs attention, and in the end it really adds value for recipients. On the other hand, if it only grabs our attention and leaves us with nothing or, even worse than before, in the end, it just leaves us with a bad feeling, a bad taste, it is not remarkable at all.

If we share something truly remarkable, then the outcome can only be positive: interested people get the opportunity to enjoy the value of it. If what we share is not remarkable, it may be catchy but not valuable, then the effect is not that people wouldn't engage, but rather the ones with whom we engage are probably people who resonate with that message, maybe not our best message.

Hence, we have to know who we want to engage first. Mainly we must clarify and decide about the buyer's persona, the ideal client we want to attract, and then operate a fine-tuning of communication according to what we understand about the buyer persona's register in our day-to-day work/learning process.

Although it appears relatively easy to decide what strategy and who the buyer persona is in order to focus on them, it can be very challenging. Choosing a strategy, is a pattern of long-term decisions. It is often said that is like getting married: decide to avoid everyone else and focus on one partner only![†]

The same is true of deciding upon the buyer's persona: to get rid of everyone else and focus on just one kind of person—deciding, consciously,

---

* Godin, S., *Purple Cow*, Penguin Books, 2005.
[†] Unknown author.

to not care about any other opportunities and stay focused on making the best of that one.

What Is Leads Generation?

Leads generation implies doing what allows us to become extremely interesting for those personas, for example, talking and discussing on what they care about, that we also care. Saying something remarkable to them becomes easier, as there is nothing that can be remarkable to everyone, but anything can be extremely remarkable for a more focused audience.

Hence, the essence of leads generation is to get in contact with people who are getting in touch with our brand, the logic behind that is: if someone is interested in what we propose, specific content of ours among the huge amount of available content, then he or she could be someone who is truly interested in the specifics of our own matter. How much and how deeply he or she is captivated is something that must be unveiled.

The funnel concept can have:

1. A hard approach, which is to get immediately in touch with that person to pursue a sale;
2. A softer approach, which is to let that person know more, search more, discover more content that relates to the topic and then engage him or her in a conversation (often referred as "marketing of permission").

None of these two approaches is wrong per se, sometimes we just observe:

■ The first approach is taken when the audience is smaller, or the business is in its initial stage or there are survival problems. If the need to sell is higher, then the strategy is focused on acting immediately;
■ The second approach is more common when a business has a wider audience, is much more settled and focuses on selecting the right clients more than any possible client.

But the job is not done yet. Starting a conversation with someone is just a first step into the waters of a relationship. With this starts the sequence of moments of truth, where the relationship matters—sometimes—more than the object.

How an LG Funnel Works

The person who enters into the funnel of engagement can be led to discover more relevant content that provides her or him with more valuable resources, testing and discovering the person's eagerness on the matter.

The standard methodology of a funnel consists of content anyone can freely benefit from; it then requires people to qualify themselves, depending on the relevance of the proposed content but also by the industry habits—the person's qualification spans from a simple mailbox address to a more complete request of details. Lately, the trend is to reduce the engagement bar, not really to pave the way for more contacts, which is actually against the purpose of selecting ideal clients, but in the awareness of a possible disengagement of also perfect-fit prospects. People's habits change, the trend is to lessen the engagement effort and everyone expects this: even perfectly motivated, fit-ideal prospects can disentangle themselves from the engagement funnel if they perceive a greater effort than its expected outcome value.

Free content can be just the content of a website or a specific topic-focused document; to proceed further and get something even more valuable, the qualification should allow the company to collect data and engage in the conversation.

While keeping the balance between freely available value sharing and return of information is important, it is actually a fine-line border that strongly depends on the value perception of the solution. To recall a previously seen concept: the more mission-critical a solution is, the more anyone really interested in it will be ready to pay a price for any valuable information over it.

Pay-in price is a broader concept, it can effectively be worth to pay a consultancy fee in order to get it in the most suitable way, or just leave an email address to get access to some valuable information rather than browse around to search for what can just be found freely.

The less painful the need, the less effort is acceptable to find a solution that relieves the problem. "Effort" here also means time. How long should you browse around to collect enough information to make the perfect decision when a solution ready for you is just one click away? (No matter if, to get this benefit, you store your credit card data in their system and you could probably pay a lower price somewhere else for it.)

Once the person engages in some conversation, the two approaches unleash the potential of the contact, but they also unveil the organisation's culture.

Sell Now

"We are sure people that entered the funnel are clients. They are looking to buy, they need a solution as they have the pain, hence we contact them to start discussing the deal: we start selling. If we don't, they buy somewhere else."

The approach to sell now has its reasons to still be in place: if it is designed by a well-aware management who is conscious of the implications of it and the assumptions behind that decision are all constantly verified, then fine: it is a working method that serves specific needs of clients.

The organisation's reasons can include:

■ Value of the object
■ Value perceived by clients
■ Use's function of the object
■ Standard of the industry
■ …

Some of the reasons that can be perceived are:

■ Pressure to sell
■ Poor value
■ Organisational culture sales-centric
■ …

The first pattern of reasons is totally fine: when they are well controlled by the management, they imply the use of a sell-now approach.

The second pattern of reasons shows what clients could perceive when a perfect design of the sales process, based on the previous reasons, is missing.

Help Now

"Helping is the new selling. As the buyer's journey has changed, so too has the approach of a today's salesperson. Though it sounds counterintuitive, make your first aim to help prospects in reaching their goals, -not your sales goals- a sales person can achieve both."

---

* Mertes, N., *With Buyers in Control, Helping is the New Selling*, weidert.com, 2019.

More businesses are now focusing on providing help to customers as a first move, then customers who would be searching for something more, will be already well-aware of whom can help them. Likewise, as Jay Baer wrote in 2013: focus on offering free service to everyone with the aim of nurturing an audience it will support your brand awareness.*

Under this paradigm, the *help-now* approach makes sense: let that person know more, search more, discover more content that matters to the topic and then engage him or her in a conversation. Let them discover among your free content anything that can help them in making a step forward. By doing that you can qualify them, track their journey and pair them with the Buyer Persona you already defined.

If they match, then they are real prospects with whom making business will come almost organically.

The organisational culture of a *help-now* approach can be perceived as:

■ Valuing the client
■ Having the mission to provide solutions
■ Offering value for money
■ …

An advantage that people can exploit is to get free help and not proceed any further. On top of it, this method can probably become quite expensive.

People who perceive the solution as critical may wish to get support in order to learn about the solution itself and they also need to qualify the provider before proceeding. Once those points are reached, trusting the provider to put in place the solution will come.

If people are keen to take advantage of the free knowledge, but are not really committed to paying for it, there isn't much we can do. Imagine if you would have engaged them in a sales process, or even worse in a deal, just to discover that they did not value your product/service enough to pay for it, but rather they were only there to grab something for free.

Here the qualification is in place. Anyone who just wishes to take free advantage doesn't match the Buyer Persona (for now). It would be then much better to save resources by not engaging that person and focusing on ones who do. However, we do accept that nobody exactly knows if, over time, today's wrong person can change the situation and become the ideal client we want on board. Hence, offering free help and knowledge is either

---

* Baer, J., *Youtility, Why Smart Marketing Is about Help not Hype*, Penguin Books, 2013.

a qualification tool to avoid bad resource allocation and an investment in future relationships that can, eventually, mature.

The Buyer Persona

We can see how all the paradigms depicted till now are strongly based on two pillars:

■ The purchasing process modelling
■ The buyer persona(s) definition

The buyer's value perspective about the solution matters on the purchasing process they wish to perform. If the sales process defines the way in which providers sell, its design is intended for the typical buyer: the buyer persona. But the same solution can have different values for different uses, as they totally depend on the client's purposes, the value/effort perception will vary accordingly. It implies that buyers will stick to the sales process as long as they match with the expected buyer persona. If they differ from that character, they wish to buy following their own agenda.

Hence, the buyer persona of each product/service is the most important parameter to take into account when we define either the marketing effort—what engages people—or the leads generation—how to engage them. And, last but not the least, how they buy—the sales process.

The process to define the buyer personas is probably one of the most complex and important duties of marketing. An effective description of the different buyer personas, as we have just seen, empowers the whole process: from a greater engagement to an improved effectiveness of the sales process.

A poor definition can lead to taking onboard problems that cannot easily be traced back to that strategic mistake.

Some of the issues an organisation can experience when they lack a proper picture of their optimal buyer persona are as follows:

■ Lack of engagement
  – A high marketing effort that does not create enough traffic.
■ Poor leads generation
  – People do not respond positively either to *sell-now* or *help-now* approaches.

▪ Scarce conversion rate
  – Among marketing qualified people, the conversion rate is still lower than expected.
▪ Highly troubled sales process
  – Salespeople have to apply a massive effort to close deals.
▪ High level of complaints and refunds
  – Customers appear difficult to satisfy, after sales complaints are usual, as requests for refunds or court cases can be above the industry average.
▪ Rarity of reviews and referrals
  – Customers who refer to a satisfactory purchase are scattered, the self-started positive reviews of the experience can be infrequent. While "haters" are more commonly prone to leave bad reviews.
▪ Economics and financial struggle
  – The organisation can experience EBITDA shrinking, a lower ROI and difficulties accessing investors and funding sources.

As we can see there are many possible effects, it is not a rule that they all will happen and their magnitude will always be dramatic. But when they are in place, it is worth investigating in this direction. Also on how are strategic decisions, including deciding the ideal-client, have been taken?

Businesses that have discovered their best buyers, and can define them precisely, report a superior performance pattern.

How to distinguish between many possible clients and which of them are more likely to get your services is "the" business problem. The issue that every business faces is to determine a valuable and relevant audience, big enough to be a market but narrow enough to be defined by common features and needs.

Each time the management describes a relevant feature of the ideal-client, it excludes a wide chunk of people who do not show that feature. Any critical need to address excludes anyone who does not feel that as a critical point. Any function of use relevant for the value perceived erases dozens if not thousands of possible clients. The more narrowly we define it, the fewer people will fit into it. Hence, the need to define the relevant *pain* that affects a wide-enough audience of people (or businesses) to be a market.

To lead the process of defining the Buyer Persona in a business-to-business (B2B) market, we suggest an enquiring method to define what are the most important client's traits.

It relies on four parameters that lead to understanding the customer's knowledge that are paramount to shape the relationship. We can define it as the WHWT acronym. That here is not a dog.*

WHWT is about understanding the client's specific situation and needs:

- What do they do
- How do they do it
- Why they do it
- To whom they do it

Gathering information by this simple method enables us to define how we can work with that counterpart.

What do they do

It tells us if what they do might benefit from our solution(s).

How do they do what they do

Clarify if their processes, methodologies and beliefs fit with our solution(s) or eventually they are ahead of it or, instead, far behind it. In the latter case, it could be more beneficial to adopt our solution, while the former suggests we can't add much value to their processes.

Why they do what they do

Here we can grasp their intentions, what do they believe they are good at and what kind of value they want to bring to their own clients. What their values are and how we fit into their vision of the world.

To whom they do what they do

If we understand their end-users and their clients, we can better figure out what kind of value our counterpart can create for them, why they choose our counterpart and the real positioning our counterpart owns in their market. Then we can figure how our solution(s) can help them in creating more value to their users and clients.

---

* See West Highland White Terrier.

To enable your buyer persona definition process, we suggest the extraordinary job done by Strategyzer, ignited by Alex Osterwalder.*

What we can report is that the concept of the buyer persona is still not widely adopted nor fully understood. It seems that many organisations are afraid to cut away wide clusters of potential buyers only because they are slightly less sensitive to some parameters, like the pain and the urgency, or they are too price-sensitive, it means those clients are less keen to pay a higher price for any solution aimed to solve a problem as they do not perceive such problem as painful. As a result, those organisations are still engaging many different kinds of buyers by nurturing wider audiences in the hope of getting more traffic, and they do it by avoiding a focused communication to one addressable need. Doing so, they also undermine their positioning and it results as less relevant, first of all for the most interesting cluster of possible clients, but ultimately for all of possible clients. This implies that the value perceived by each of them is lower than what was planned by the organisation, and the solution can result in a fierce opposition to the pricing. It might result in a higher churn rate than expected, and a wider request of price reduction, discounts and gratuities made by salespeople. Last but not least, to make things less easy, we can have many Buyer Personas for the same product/service, as long as we differentiate the sales process (and sales conditions) in accordance with each different buyer persona we are going to engage. It may imply the need to create different communication registers that should be delivered to the right prospect.

Prospect and Opportunities

When people, now called leads, are qualified on the marketing funnel, they pass through to the sales process.

MQL (Marketing Qualified Lead) and SQL (Sales Qualified Lead) are two qualification processes. The first is related to the leads generation funnel:

> *"A marketing qualified lead is a lead who has been deemed more likely to become a customer compared to other leads. This qualification is based on what web pages a person has visited, what they've downloaded, and similar engagement with the business's content.*

---

* strategyzer.com

A company's lead-intelligence is often informed by closed-loop analytics. Sit down with your sales managers to determine which demographics, activities and behaviors make for an MQL at your company.

Based on the lead definitions you create, you can assign point values for various MQL qualifications in order to form the basis of your lead scoring system.

*This will ensure your sales team is delivered high-quality leads so they can improve their productivity, while Sales and Marketing remain aligned in their goals."**

We already have discussed SQL in Chapter 3, but it is useful to recall it here again: qualification of leads is like a fine-mesh filtering where prospects become the ones who are closest to the buyer persona the organisation has defined. The output of these two combined qualification stages are people who are truly interested in purchasing the solution. If the organisation will be the preferred one, it will probably be one of the sales team goals. These people are now prospects and they represent "sales opportunities." More often defined as "deals," that are abstract entities that include the object of purchasing (products or services), value, timing, participants like stakeholders, nature of the agreement and conditions.

In many CRM the term "deals" is used to refer about entities to which salespeople address their effort along the sales process management; deals are folders, containers where data, activities and performance, that are useful for reporting and forecasting on the sales process itself are recorded.

From Leads Generation to CRM

The output of leads generation are people, qualified contacts: someone who, at a certain point, has been interested in some content that we proposed.

People who, whether they completed the purchasing process or not, are still relevant contacts for us. From the leads generation process, they have been moved into the sales process by evaluating if they were in the right time and situation to become clients.

---

* Kusinitz, S., *The Definition of a Marketing Qualified Lead*, Hubspot, 2018.

Whatever would be the end of those processes, what to do with those contacts is something the organisation has to define. The CRM, here intended as the repository of contact information, events and interaction, now has its full role. Firstly, it is to be noted that each business and industry has its own habits, style and ways to keep the relationship open between clients and providers.

The trend to engage clients in a continuous conversation can be more successful for some kinds of businesses, whereas it may be totally unacceptable for others. However, a (possible) conversation is definitely a valuable point of touch to nurture audiences of potential new or repetitive clients.

The logic of the CRM is what matters the most: deciding what to do is the real critical point of a CRM management, not how to do it.

The mission to create segmentation in the CRM tool has no complications—later in this book we will see it—every pre-built platform has it included, while CRM developed upon fully customisable platforms should be planned to include it. Any professional developer who is about to design a CRM tool knows how to do it.

What matters the most is "why" the process of creating segmentation is relevant and how we can leverage it.

Let's start analysing the outcome of leads generation and sales process:

Leads Generation

Leads can be qualified (MQL) or not, qualified leads are contacts that are hypothetically among the market target, it means they may feel the pain or be aware of the problem to solve.

Here the decisions tree involves:

- Leads not qualified
- MQL: Marketing Qualified Leads
  - Passed into SP (for instance due to RFM matrix's fit)
  - Aborted

Sales Process

Leads become contacts, and they can be qualified (SQL) or not, the qualified ones are operators who are in search of a solution to their problem.

Here the decisions tree:

- Leads not qualified
- SQL: Sales Qualified Leads
  - Prospect abandoned the process (which stage)
  - Prospect not converted (at the end of process)
  - Prospect converted

Each of the above can be a segment. To each segment, we can plan a different conversation according to the business development tactics and the long-term strategy.

In order to design that, we should place some conditions:

Leads Generation

Qualification rules should be clearly defined, what qualifies a company/person as a possible client? In the MQL stage is more about general parameters: if they belong to a certain industry or type of companies... If not we better record that data.

Here the decisions tree:

I. Non-MQL
   A. Why? What reason to exclude them?
      1. Not users/not buyers
         a) Proposing to them a sort of "stay in touch" to learn might be useful? y/n
         b) Let them browse around free content knowing what they do (CRM records the web-tracking)
II. MQL
   A. Passed into Sales Process (refer to later actions)
   B. Aborted
      1. Why? What made it happen?
         a) As this output shouldn't normally happen

Sales Process

In the sales process the qualification stage (see chapter 3) selects the contacts that are ready to buy—Prospects—allowing to move them along the sales process. But it is also paramount to keep the Non-SQL contacts as an audience in the CRM loop, they might change their situation later and be qualified as prospects at any time.

Here the decisions tree:

I. Not SQL
   A. Why? What excluded them?
      1. Not ready to buy now
      2. Not in the "ideal-client" group
      3. Lack of budget
      4. Lack of pain/need
      5. Time mismatch
         a) Designing proper scenarios can help in deciding what is better to do with each of them.
            (1) For instance, time mismatch, as not ready to buy now or lack of budget/need, are those conditions that might change in future? If this is possible, then it can be good to keep open a conversation nurturing these relationships.
            (2) Did it result in prospect buying another solution in the market? If so, what can be useful to plan to do with them? Can they come back later to us? Can they feel the need for a better solution, or, once they have bought, they will never buy another one?
            (a) Delete/disengage
            (b) Come back to them in a period of time
II. SQL, Qualified Prospects
   A. Why did they abandon the process?
   B. What made the deal unsuccessful?
   C. What made them buy?
      1. For each answer, we can define what to do either in short or in long-term relationships. Each question opens several options such that each may set a conversation topic.
         a) They abandoned the process as their whole experience wasn't successful. When, what, how?
            (1) Can we learn from it? Can it be useful to offer them anything that—helping us to learn—make them feel we truly care?
         b) They abandoned it because they found another solution that fits their needs better.

  (1) What, how, why? Learn what made them decide to buy something else that can be useful for us? Are they expected to buy again (... and again)? Can we keep giving them good qualitative content waiting for them to make another purchase?

 2. If they converted, know why they did it: knowing what the decision driver was is pretty valuable information to leverage with, especially if paired with the person (company) profile (what kind of prospect he or she [or them] was?)

Based on the outcome of both the leads generation and the sales process operations, we collect valuable information to feed the later stage: the audiences nurturing.

Audiences Nurturing

We can now evaluate the possibilities connected with a growing number of contacts with whom we had some interaction and we have collected some interest or needs at a certain time.

Of course, there is the GDPR in place, it implies we can't keep running marketing campaigns without their consensus and, eventually, we have to erase any data we collected about them at any time they express this requirement.

Let's say that if it is true that getting consensus to keep bothering someone is getting harder nowadays, having someone interested in some valuable information often is not a mission impossible.

Then if it is true that end users can ask to delete any data about themselves from any company's database, not only about marketing, it is also true that it requires them to express that request and, if there is not a serious reason to ask for it: why should they do it?

Knowing what someone, a person or a company, that came in contact with us sometime in the past did/didn't do with us is relevant, not only to us but probably also for themselves. Knowing for instance the preferences of returning contacts can be useful to skip part of the qualification, or facilitate the enquiring process—with clear benefits for both parties. We are talking about returning contacts, because collecting data of clients is normal, and accepted by everyone, according to sales conditions. It is a different matter to have clients' data and use them for marketing purposes and/or exchange data with business partners. For that purpose, a specific authorisation should have been given by each client. (Refer to GDPR rule and Privacy Law wherever they are in place)

Let's imagine a business that is able to produce good, valuable, interesting content. No matter the format—written, video or audio—as long as it is viable for recipients and it is properly addressed to narrowly defined audiences, meeting their interests, and is capable of grabbing their interest and creating value to them when using that content for their personal or business purposes.

This growing style of proposing valuable content aimed at specific audiences is a powerful method that allows organisations to nurture market audiences, keep conversations open and build Brand Awareness, define their Positioning and act on their Brand Character while offering to help people with the aim of growing their clientele in number and loyalty.

It is what has also been called segmented marketing, the nurture of groups small enough to be narrowly defined but wide enough to be a valuable market segment. Differentiation is created by communication, hence the same solution can serve many different clusters and many different buyer personas as long as they truly perceive that unique value proposition they resonate with. It implies that a valuable market segment can, eventually, be divided into many smaller groups of interest where communication can be adapted to their own needs. It means either leads generation or CRM should be designed to communicate in different ways according to the audience segmentation.

Here B to B marketing takes some influence from a business-to-consumer (B to C) approach that opens many possibilities of understanding and planning a more effective marketing campaign.

Summary

Leads generation pushes contact data into the CRM and then the Sales Process can be run, thereafter the CRM segmentation and planned routines enable conversations between business and leads/prospects.

■ It seems simple when said like this! To make it effective for each business style, following its register of voice and the different possibilities, but also running qualification and sales processes for each buyer persona, can be, instead, quite complex.

■ In this chapter, we went through the leads generation stage as an element of the brand's marketing, and we discovered the importance of strategically defining the buyer persona to set the fine-tuning of the conversation, although the whole marketing approach is focused on either one client's type or on many different buyer personas.

■ About the concept of Valuable Help, we analysed what engages people and how the connection of new leads can work in its logic approach.

■ Finally, we have seen how those contact people, at the end of all processes, become audiences in the CRM, people with whom we can create, build and nurture relationships by conversation.

Chapter 5

Helping People (Customer Service)

Helping is the new selling. Therefore, providing a *good service* is paramount. What does it mean for an organisation, and how can we support this purpose? How can we leverage digital tools to enable people to work better?

The topics covered in this chapter are as follows:

1. People search for solutions
2. Communicating value through valuable service
3. Customer experience
4. Customer service IT tools

People Search for Solutions

No one wakes up in the morning saying: *"Let's go spend money."* OK, wrong, a few people may indeed do that, especially if they are married to a tycoon. But let's leave this minority aside. We know that everyone has a pattern of needs to fill, and browses around looking for solutions able to meet those needs. Therefore, people try to trade off between available resources that are scarce for definition, and possible solutions, always too many to be managed.

There is a way to assess whether a possible provider and their possible solutions can fit the seeker's requirements: get some initial experience. Even

DOI: 10.4324/9781003148388-5

if it is not directly about the solution, at least the experience helps the seeker to test the provider.

Here starts the opportunity to help people. Welcome people who come to us for just one piece of information, maybe a little help. Sometimes people who just come for a webinar, a video or some kind of content with some free benefit do not really intend to buy. Maybe they get in touch with us to ask questions they can't easily find answers to online. Or that they could find, but they didn't.

"Helping People" is more than "Customer Care," as help is offered to anyone who asks for it, no matter whether they have bought anything from us yet.

"Yet" is the point. Of course business survives by exchanging value for money, thus there is no doubt that the purpose of helping is to "convince" people to become customers. Every company wants it, but today they can choose a more gentle approach to drive sales. Even if choosing a gentle approach actually is not really just an option anymore, what we notice is that businesses that boost their capabilities in helping people show better results as a direct effect of their perceived competitive value.

We can go ahead with this simple, globally accepted concept of helping people by reporting what Jay Baer affirms: *"Haters are not your problem, ignoring them is."**

Let's analyse what Jay says:

"There are two types of complainers, each with very different motivations:

- ■ *Offstage haters. These people simply want solutions to their problems. They complain via legacy channels where the likelihood of a response is highest —phone, e-mail, and company websites. Offstage haters don't care if anyone else finds out, as long as they get answers.*
- ■ *Onstage haters. These people are often disappointed by a substandard interaction via traditional channels, so they turn to indirect venues, such as social media, online review sites, and discussion boards. Onstage haters want more than solutions —they want an audience to share their righteous indignation."*

---

* Baer, J., *Hug Your Haters: How to Embrace Complaints and Keep Your Customers*, Portfolio, 2016.

Jay answers a relevant question: why do people express such rage? The reason is often that they just want solutions. Maybe they paid for a service/product and they are not getting the expected support. They probably asked for support many times before the point they got irritated. Such a reaction can be complex to understand. Let's try to find the sense behind it. We all live in an extremely fast and stressful environment; in some ways it is also a violent time where gentle people are often ignored and good reasons are trampled on while many people prefer shortcuts to get answers that simplify the matter instead of dealing with complexity. We have all learnt that raising your voice to be heard is often more effective than asking gently. Hence good people can also be tempted to show anger, hate, because behaving gently hasn't helped them in reaching the point. Oddly you will more often find opposite opinions about haters, something like this: *"Haters are your confirmation you are doing something right."**

Well, as Jay Baer affirms: *"... 95% of customers never take the time to complain."* What we all know is that this really makes sense. Few people have time to waste, hence anyone who invests time to complain probably feels they have a big problem.

Therefore, it is a business problem to ignore complaints but it is clearly quite a problem even to manage them well. Companies that set a methodology in place using digital tools (CRM) to enable them in dealing with complaints can better deal with the challenge to stay up to date with the social changes happening around them. Nowadays it is much more socially acceptable when people show hate, anger and attack brands for their *"customer care below the expectations."* This can affect the brand's reputation, and knowing this, people use it as a weapon to persuade customer care departments of brands to pay attention to them. It is a great opportunity for brands that want to excel in customer service, to develop better customer care and empower it to deal with clients better than the level that other brands can perform, this is possible and not too hard to achieve. Opportunities arise where market expectations change and competitors do not change fast enough, hence being able to appreciate these trends and setting out a better proposal in the market may pay off. If customer care, or our own way to help people, is seen as a marketing opportunity instead of an unavoidable cost, then its value will shift, and so will its outcome. When companies embrace the opportunity to help their audiences, their brand becomes popular as people seek help to navigate the complexity and chaos of their

---

* Wright, A., *36 Things I Have Learned About Haters*, ART+Marketing, Medium, 2016.

lives. Even a little help about a product or service that smooths their day is something that people love.

Communicating Value Through Valuable Service

In fact there is more than that; brands that offer help—no matter what—can turn annoyed, unhappy customers into advocates. Why does this happen? People who have a need, who are looking for solutions, get annoyed when their search is stuck in a dead-end. Help that, resolves their situation, actually sorts it out, and also redeems the waste of time (hence value) they placed into what seemed a wrong decision—the decision to believe a provider and eventually buy a solution, only to find out that not only can it not solve the problem, but it has now added another problem to their life. And the more the solution is felt to be critical, the more urgent it is and thus the more they feel irritated.

Getting value back into their purchasing process, also when it can actually be much longer than expected, means they not only can restore their trust in the provider, but they also get more value than expected. They turn a loss into a winning situation. And even if they can't achieve the solution they wanted, at least the help makes them feel the loss as part of the learning process required to reach the expected solution. The outcome is no longer a loss, but a learning experience.

A company, a brand, which is able to deliver such value, even if the problem was not created by a product/service of theirs, is a brand that demonstrates its focus on the relationship with the audience—not just with existing customers but with anyone who can become a customer in future.

You have probably heard about the 89-year-old man who was stuck at home in Pennsylvania due to terrible weather while his daughter was struggling to find a store that would deliver him some food. She finally found Trader Joe's, which took care of the problem and went out delivering food to her old father. And oddly, Trader Joe's didn't want to be paid. The staff truly acted like any human who cares about other humans. People experience the company's own real intentions, hence customers reward them with loyalty. The story went viral as an effect of the employees' true intent; as a result, new shoppers considered the shop. If Trader Joe's had done this with the intention of going viral and getting more clients, that would probably have resulted in other clients forming a negative opinion about the company.

> *"You must think in the language of the problems you solve for your customers. Focus on the customer relationship, not the transaction and add value each time you interact with them."**

Ada Okoli's article in the Zoovü company's blog lists some real gems about why and how helping people pays off. The subtle secret is that intentions are not for sale.

Customer Experience

> *"To create positive experiences, you need to stand up for the customers and have their best interests at heart. Help customers that want to be helped.*
> *Even if it doesn't win you a sale immediately, it places you high in the customer's good book."†*

Some entrepreneurs could probably be more sceptical about the pay-off that nice gestures can really get, while they are scared about losing reputation. Whether the driver is to not get bad reviews or to get more clients later, the true intentions are what people will perceive. It can be difficult to draw the line between charity and real, genuine intent to help while still doing business.

This is not something that can be planned; the movement should come naturally inside a proper, healthy business. It can be really difficult to be helpful when your business is going bankrupt or even when you are just struggling under competition.

But the service offered, as well as the whole customer's experience, become a signal of value that people perceive. Credible businesses are capable of creating value for their clients. It is something good businesses are capable of putting in place before it is too late.

In a market where customers are more aware, more educated, more informed, businesses can sustain and flourish by focusing on the customer experience, leveraging their CRM to propose content to their audiences that helps them in their quest for solutions. Creating a unique relationship that

---

* Okoli, A., *Helping Is the New Selling – With Buyers In Control, The Definition Of Selling Needs An Update*, ZOOVÜ blog, 2017.
† Okoli, A., 2017, ibidem.

helps create reasonable value even before the purchasing process, and even in case of a non-successful sales attempt, keeps the relationship healthy is paramount nurturing people's experience. As we have seen, unqualified leads can also come back under a more suitable framework, thereby enabling both parties to benefit from the long-term relationship.

How to use the CRM tool to provide help and simultaneously to collect data from contact people and how to leverage it to keep conversation afloat is something that we will see later in more detail, but under the CRM strategy it is important that a business that is planning the implementation of CRM or its revamp focuses on the preparation of the "What we want to achieve with the CRM."

Our purpose here is to highlight the possible connection and the value of "Helping People" as a better approach than just "customer care," in the CRM logic, where the effort to help people allows businesses to leverage their CRM tool while they also enhance their audiences.

Business and Technology Strategies Must Become Indistinguishable

I'm pleased to ask Omar Fogliadini his point of view: " - It's a moment of truth: technology has sustained us through the pandemic and now it continues to redefine the way we work, live and interact with each other and with businesses.

Many organisations appear to be out of sync, sometimes too rigid or slow moving, at a pace that is definitely slower than the consumer's changing pace. Consumer's expectations have become liquid across different product and service categories. They appear no longer comparing their brand's experiences between two different companies in the same space. Rather, they make comparisons between their usual day by day brand's experience and the mobile service provider with a best-in-class airline, or even a digital giant, design & tech-driven player such as Airbnb.

Today's consumers need, and they expect even more of, a simple, fast, and meaningful experience delivered in a way that is responsive in the moment they live.

Many companies lack the digital tools needed to deliver on consumer's changing needs. They are still reliant on 10-year-old systems and inherently react slowly with backward-looking and incomplete data. These tools can be unable to translate the massive volume of customer data and signals into immediate actions and smart decisions that drive customer acquisition, wallet share, retention. But probably the need to embrace new tools also depends on other dynamics that organisations find hard to overcome, the environment is changing at a speed that giant and slow pace organisations can't really face. The more they try to do that by engaging themselves into big projects to update their digital infrastructure the less they can react fast enough. This is why medium organisations can actually have a great competitive advantage: they are not too small to lack in resources and skills and not too big to be stuck into dynamics that can hold them back from acting.

Enabling the User-First, Omnichannel Experience

Companies must rethink how and where they connect with consumers. The most successful companies in the post-coronavirus digital age are integrating this approach by prioritizing three elements:

1. *Availability of online purchasing capability*
2. *Ease of navigating phygital customer journeys*
3. *Seamless integration of sales support and advice capabilities.*

Experiences must be local, fast and relevant to the moment. By using big data, predictive analytics, and machine learning, companies can go from "How are we doing?" to "What do customers want next?" This customer-focused, data-driven approach will allow companies to unlock efficiencies, predict customer behavior, track satisfaction drivers, anticipate churn, and flag opportunities to turn loyalty into profitability.

Sync the Tech, Data and Human Agenda

"Phygital" is poised to take the best components from the digital experience such as immediacy, immersion, and speed and meshes it with physical products and personal interactions. Now, with the added need to bridge social distancing, digital tools can step in to minimise unnecessary human interactions whilst boosting a sense of connection.

Whilst we may be constrained to social distance, social shopping is ramping up to transform our retail world into an exciting experience. Digital marketers can no longer afford to have separate strategies for retail and eCommerce. The entire shopping experience has to be multi-layered and interlinked if tomorrow's consumers are to enjoy an improved user experience.-"*

---

* Fogliadini, O., *LifeData*, 2021.

Customers' Service IT Tools

If we keep the classic, already well-known, designation of customer service or customer care to talk about the topic and digital tools that empower this function, we can better understand the framework. Still, the purpose remains to help people in their solution search who could, eventually or possibly, be our customers.

Let's define two stages:

1. Helping by providing resources for self-service fruition
2. Helping by direct support and assistance

Under the first stage, to nurture audiences, what matters is the creation of qualitative contents by focusing on the buyer persona's need and style. Let the content be available for free for the first engagement, then foster the next level of engagement by providing even more knowledge-based content to registered users.

Content is the value, but its availability and searchability are key to making people benefit from it. No value can be obtained from a hidden gem, while a lot of value can be derived from a good enough article which is easy to locate. The real challenge is to stand out from the crowd by establishing authority, giving the audience confidence about the intrinsic value.

It has often been said that content should be "awesome," but probably more than that the content should be authoritative, easy to find and then (possibly) good.

The method to make helpful content available is to nurture any media channel and search engine optimisation so that anyone approaching the matter will find it.

This is the marketing function that, in the digital world, is run by specific tools that are the marketing automation platforms. The same kind of tool we have seen in leads generation, where we mentioned content in a generic way. Here we join the two: promote contents that help people!

The second stage, that is, helping people by direct support and assistance, is a much more labour-intensive activity. For this very reason, it can be a problem but also brings opportunities. One problem comes from the necessity of running it using personnel, as solutions like using ChatBots as automatic responders do not seem to have been able to match the human touch yet. They can support the process, especially leading people when it comes to suggesting any related content. The function of ChatBots is then pretty useful when they are *transactional* ChatBots, as pre-designed automation that provides customers with a fixed set of choices.* Customers select a relevant option for what they want to achieve, then the chatbot guides them through the process. More complex is the case of a conversational chatbot, designed to understand and respond to a conversation in a natural, human-like manner—something that seems not fully achieved—. For this reason, the chatbot experience is debated; it surely improves speed, but can be not pleasant for customers who can't find a solution. Hence, what to choose between machine and human interaction is the wrong question for a company to ask.†

ChatBots would anyway be an improvement on the dreadful, once-fashionable FAQs page. The idea that someone would be happy to waste time on a FAQ page is just so old-fashioned, and it can lead businesses to the bottom of the customer's experience ranking nowadays.

The solutions applied till now, the call centre department, didn't solve the problem; then it is still clear that call centres run by customer service personnel can be highly expensive and often demonstrate low levels of efficiency. Outsourcing those workforces achieved the goal of cost reduction but, on the other hand, it left this mission-critical function led by a productivity driver to be managed from outside the business "owner's" control, who therefore cannot exert the genuine intention of helping people.

The opportunity comes from the possibility to deliver first-class interactions, best assistance, valuable support and help to everyone in need, something that definitely has a paramount impact on the value of the business. Technology definitely helps: customer support platforms are tools situated alongside the CRM and the marketing automation, and their role spans from the engagement stage to the after-sales support stage. And for this reason, they have a very special role in the business processes. They are not CRM even if their function can be integrated into a CRM platform, or they can be run independently by a more specialised tool that does not need to include the CRM.

The CRM remains at the core of the architecture and is where data are stored; integrated service platforms use and combine that data, also feeding the CRM with conversational events.

---

* Bullock, M., *Chatbots, are they the Panacea for Customer Experience?*, Medium, 2019.
† Jones, T., *Man vs. Machine: Chatbots and the Future of Customer Service*, customerthink.com, 2017.

Technology today allows such an enhancement in service management that was pretty much impossible in the past. A company like Rapha Sportswear manages a traffic of 13000+ service tickets per month with 40 agents, while Lonely Planet hits only 5000+ tickets per month with 27 agents.

The solution for a medium enterprise can be to implement a dedicated customer service tool, integrating it with a CRM that supports the sales process. Eventually, the organisation can also use a third element such as a conversational database to store data garnered from the chat, ticketing and all other conversation channels like text messaging, WhatsApp, Messenger and social media.

The result will be a system that provides real-time information on any interaction between each client and anyone in the company at any time. It tracks the specific client position, such as if he or she is in the sales process or included in an audience or is a happy client or whatever else. It also enables developing detailed reporting about the interaction trends and customers' journey.

The logic behind it relies on the specialisation of tools and the flexibility to decide which among all the available tools better fits the business requirements for each function. We believe among many tools each organisation should select the one that enables the business to run the processes in its own fashion and does not force the company to change its processes to match the tool. Therefore, choosing the right service platform that enables the service teams in working efficiently on their own processes can already be a challenge. Then there is the difficulty of implementing a CRM that fits the business sales process, either a business-to-business, business-to-consumer or business-to-business-to-consumer business model, with complex or simple, straightforward sales actions.

After this, we must also consider the complexity of the selection of an appropriate marketing automation, another specific tool that should enable the content's searchability in every channel and support the process of leads generation by feeding the CRM and taking control of contacts' behaviour on the website as well as interactions with proposed contents.

To limit the system architecture analysis just here, we can see how the complexity of each tool and its mission-critical functions lead to two possibilities: one big tool that runs everything, or a composed mix of different integrated tools. We will come back to these options later in this book, as they entail different approaches and also a complex competencies pattern available inside the company.

The Customer Service Vision 2020

(Market research from Zendesk)

*The Past Year Brought Swift and Unprecedented Change**

Not only did a global pandemic transform the way we live, collaborate and connect, but economic and social disruptions forced customers to re-examine their values and what they expect from the companies they do business with.

We've been on a long march toward a digital-first world. One where all interactions between company and customer, and company and employee transcend physical spaces. While the concept of digital transformation is certainly nothing new, never before has it been so vital for all companies to push ahead or risk playing catch up. Virtually overnight, shelter-in-place orders drove commerce almost exclusively online, forced companies of all sizes to contend with the future of their workplaces and set new baselines around what customers expect.

Against the backdrop of dizzying change and record high engagement, companies have had to adapt in ways that they never thought possible, at a time when the customer experience has only become more important. Customers want speed and convenience, but they're also seeking empathy and commitment to the core issues that they care about. It's a high bar, at a particularly challenging time, but companies that invest in solutions to help them work smarter and adapt quickly to evolving customer preferences will be better prepared to handle any uncertainty that lies ahead.

More conversation leads to better relationships.† This is true in life and in customer service. With friends, it's easy to begin a conversation on Facebook and to pick it up in person, but in customer service, it can be a lot more challenging. Multiply the number of customers with the number of communication channels available and the ease with which customers can communicate on their mobile devices, and suddenly there's a lot to track. Without a unified support system, customer conversations become siloed in different tools or software, creating a disjointed customer experience. These days, it is as important to answer customers as it is to track when and where they contact you, and to pick up each conversation exactly where the last one left off.

---

* Zendesk, *Redefining CX for a New Era*, Zendesk, 2021.
† Zendesk, *Better Customer Experience with Omni-Channel Engagement*, Zendesk, 2021.

The Changing Definition of Good Service

The digital economy and the rapid adoption of technology have changed everything about the customer experience. Consumers rely on word of mouth as much as ever, but often from review sites, from people they don't know. They're also interacting with companies before and after the point of sale to ask questions before making a commitment. There's more information at hand, leading to more informed decision making, which is great—except that the multitude of consumer questions places a higher demand for resources on a business. The more a business meets consumer expectations, the higher these expectations climb. It may sound daunting, but consumers are raising the bar and helping all of us to provide better customer service. Research in Zendesk's Customer Experience Trends Report 2020 revealed how high the customer loyalty bar has become. Consumers expect to reach brands on more channels than ever and demand better resolution times across every touch-point of engagement.

While traditional contact touch-points, such as email and the phone, remain important, Benchmark research revealed that patience for response

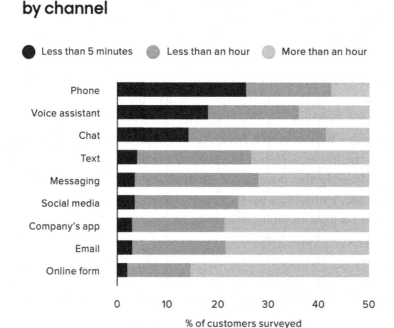

Figure 5.1   **What customers expect in terms of answering time.**

times is shortening, as 51% of respondents expect a response in under five minutes on the phone and 28% expect the same on live chat. The immediacy of a conversation on new and emerging channels like social media and text messaging can raise customer expectations for speedy responses over traditional channels, such as email and the phone. And speed is an increasingly important factor in how customers choose to contact your business.

In fact, findings also show that half of customers choose a channel based on how fast they need a response, and half say that they like to contact customer service over the same channels that they use to interact with families and friends. The details are in the data: Delivering fast responses on your customers' channels of choice affects customer satisfaction and loyalty directly.

However, despite customers' expectations, most companies aren't incorporating channels other than phone and email. In fact, fewer than 30% offer chat, social messaging, bots or communities—key channels for quick and easy communication.

Help Your Team Meet Customers' Expectations

It's possible to give customers what they want, but you'll need an engagement model that allows you to move with the customer, and to shift in time with the customer's requirements, preferences and changing expectations. You'll also need a solution that does more for you. Solving a ticket is good, but uncovering the root problem is better. Excellent service isn't just about resolving a ticket—it's about getting to know your customer.

A good way to get to know your customers better is to give them choices for how and when to interact with your business. It's not just that some customers prefer the phone, while others gravitate towards self-service—it's more that customers prefer to have options. Based on the complexity of the question, how convenient it is to find help and the context—who the customer is, what they're doing and how urgently they need an answer—the right channel will often make itself apparent.

The ability to offer seamless service via all channels, or to turn channels on or off strategically as you grow, allows businesses of all sizes to meet consumers' expectations. The key is to enable your customers to have natural conversations with your business, regardless of how or when they contact you.

CX teams generally aren't offering channels beyond phone and email

- Only 28% offer a knowledge base
- Fewer than 30% offer chat, social messaging, in-app messaging, bots or communities

Teams aren't planning to add real-time channels that their customers want

- Since fast responses and resolutions are customers' top priorities
- Only 35% of Benchmark companies take an omni-channel approach

Figure 5.2   Trends and existing situation of Customer Care contact management.

This involves connecting all channels so that agents can have continuous conversations, with access to history and context, to give customers the effortless, fast and personalised experiences that they expect.

Let Customers Say It Once, and Once Only

A hallmark of excellent service is to make it easy for a customer to contact a business and to get help. However, this is a sticking point for many businesses offering support across channels. When channels are served by different agents using different systems, customers have to explain their problem—and every step they've already taken to resolve the problem—to everyone they talk to.

This has been the way of things for a long time, but it's no longer the status quo. In fact, 71% of customers expect companies to collaborate internally so that they don't have to repeat themselves.

To deliver on customer expectations, support teams will need a connective layer of tissue that gives agents the context they need to have natural conversations with customers, such as the customer's email address, account type or the reason why they last contacted you. With this, customers can get the personalised experiences that they expect, and agents won't have to spend time asking the same questions over and over again.

Customers often begin an interaction on the channel that's most convenient for them. They tend to start with self-service, by searching for an answer in your Help Centre. From there, they may initiate a chat.

The agent handling the chat should know which articles the customer has already viewed so that they don't offer the same article in response.

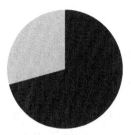

71% of customers expect
companies to collaborate
internally so that they
don't have to repeat
themselves.

Figure 5.3 Talking about User's Experience—and what customer expect.

When agents are guided by a central source of customer intelligence, they're empowered to make decisions based on data instead of intuition.

Similarly, when support is embedded into your app, there's no need to ask a customer to tell you which version and which device they're using. Agents can get to the bottom of the problem sooner, and with the help of AI, see how likely the customer is to be satisfied with the interaction, as well as take steps to ensure a positive experience.

Connected Conversations Lead to More Insight

The gains in productivity go far beyond removing repetition. Fostering natural, connected conversations across touch-points allows businesses to meet customers where they are and glean intelligence from each interaction.*

Summary

When we talk about customer care, most managers and entrepreneurs just link this concept to an expensive army of call centre young people who have to answer 24/7 to dummy customers who didn't understand how to use the product.

In this chapter we discussed a little about the IT matter and how to make it with a digital tool, but mainly we challenged that paradigm:

---

* Zendesk, *Better Customer Experience with Omni-Channel Engagement*, Zendesk, 2021.

■ People who contact the companies are in search of solutions, they ask for help.

■ Companies that receive requests of any type have the fantastic opportunity to engage prospects and existing clients in a conversation, providing support, help and ultimately value which are more relevant to attract customers than any kind of leads generation.

■ Boosting the customer experience to retain them is also part of the customer care stage mission. But it can also be a fantastic channel to test effects on clients' experience of any change or improvement.

■ IT tools that enable omnichannel conversations are now in their early stage, but they become more reliable everyday. Such tools can be really useful even if they are still complex to implement.

■ Among many available platforms that provide "customer care" we suggest selecting carefully as the implementation is the greatest investment and the functions should be fully integrated to CRM.

■ A possible system architecture can be with a conversational database that provides storage and data exchange with CRM and other software.

Case Study

Giardini, an Italian Case of Success

www.leatheredgepaint.com
Enrico Giardini, Tenente di Vascello, 1976

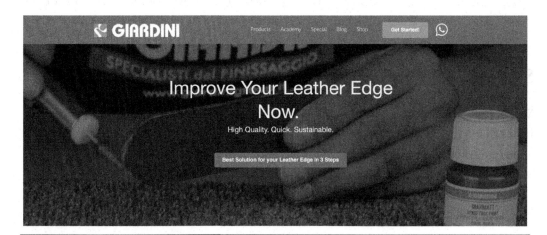

Figure 5G01   Giardini website.

In 2014 Giardini started producing a brand new product: a leather edge paint.

Enrico, who joined the family business in 2004, was ready to take care of it. It was a blind leap as the business was in chemicals for leather, focused on shoe producers according to the industrial district of Civitanova Marche.

The new product was intended to go outside the shoe makers' market, providing a growing industry of leather bags and accessories producers with the value of a better finishing of their products' edge.

The Story

There was little experience in the company and only a few clients were active in the leather bag and accessories market at the time. The market was already served by 5 big players, but Giardini Group decided to take the challenge and prepared a market test. If you never try, you never fail.

The first website, simple and cost effective, was built by Enrico who has a background in electronics and served in the army as a navy lieutenant. The coup of luck Enrico had was to find the best domain name that wasn't already taken. The challenge starts. First results are encouraging; search engine optimisation tests show a high ranking for the search engine word *"leather edge paint."* Enrico decides to embrace a high positioning, high price for best-in-class customer service.

His preferred readings included *Steve Jobs: The Exclusive Biography* by Walter Isaacson. Enrico embraces the "stay foolish" sense of purpose and accordingly commits himself with addicted attention to a customer-centric strategy.

His first CRM is a magnetic board where names of prospects are coloured Post-its, supported by magnets. Stages are vertical columns. The first year he managed to sell 100K euro worth of the brand new paint. The growth is mainly organic, later paired with some social campaigning. The presence in industry fair trades around the world is still one of the main public inbound media, and Enrico understands the importance of placing your face on it. He starts acting directly in the promotional video published on the web; clients who meet him at fair trades recognise him and some want to take a selfie with Enrico. He becomes a celebrity. While Enrico understands the importance of data mining and business intelligence, he also pushes to develop better communication: the challenge is to transfer the sense of the UX, what the client can expect from the whole purchasing experience.

Enrico has more luck while interviewing some candidates for the position of sales assistant. Enrico suddenly understands the great value of a young graduate when he has already given his word to another, also a very good one. Enrico takes the risk, telling her: *"If you are able to prepare the HubSpot certification within one day, the job position is yours."* Enrico knows how hard the challenge is, probably too hard to be achieved in 24 hours. But she made it, in the afternoon she called Enrico and got the job. Now Enrico found himself with two young, well-educated girls, both committed to the challenge. It is a bit of a risk to hire two people when you were planning for one. But entrepreneurs are that kind of people. First jump, then build the airplane.

One morning Enrico arrives at the office and finds 50 new orders from 50 brand new clients from South Korea. He has never been there and doesn't even speak Korean. But someone in that country has posted in a local social media group a video talking about the Giardini Leather Paint just the day before. Enrico understands the power of video and invests resources in that channel with more commitment. Giardini videos explain how to do it—how to use the paint, what's the secret for the best application—for those clients who aim for the best results, they are pure gold. Enrico is committed to finding the right register to talk to his audience; he is struggling to define the buyer persona and while doing that he makes mistakes and takes wrong turns. But tests and trials are the best way to learn. Measuring it by data intelligence is the key for the learning process and correcting the direction.

Pricing has been another tough decision as the existing bigger players offer their products at half of Giardini's price. To be able to justify pricing twice the competitors is often felt an unachievable challenge by entrepreneurs in any industry. Even more so for existing markets with established competitors. Enrico didn't start by calculating the production cost; he set the bar high in order to justify the whole customer service effort and the extreme attention to every detail. No matter what it requires, nothing can be left unplanned. Enrico didn't play to lose, he played to win. It must be mentioned that the typical costs for the revenue structure of a small artisan producing £20,000 per year worth of finished goods are £6,000 of raw leather and £50 of Giardini Paint.

CRM and Leads Generation

Enrico kept the magnetic board as long as he learnt the method, a kanban visual rendering of the leads generation and sales process. After learning in HubSpot academy how to run leads generation via marketing automation, Enrico made the leap of faith in investing in the business. He already had one-year records that showed him the market opportunity and its trends, which he decided to grasp. In the Giardini business model, leads generation matters for the greatest part of the whole process of sales. Of course, it also requires tracking conversations and stages when prospects are in the decision-making stage. The great benefit is that human interactions can be limited and client direct contact is not the most used activity of sales. In this case, clients mainly get in touch with the mailing automation that has been set as a human touch messaging platform instead of a fancy template.

The process is not too complicated. Engaging the client with the proper communication style clarifies if he or she fits the buyer persona, then a demo of the product follows which provides the client with a free of charge test. Once the test is over the client is ready to decide. Then nurturing the contact can be a softer activity; no need to push for a sale.

The great benefit of a reliable, fully customisable marketing automation was to free up time from repetitive tasks, enabling Enrico and his team to focus on the harder challenges.

Best Achievements

Giardini in 2020 served 72 countries and even clients such as Google and Apple along with thousands of small entrepreneurs producing leather goods

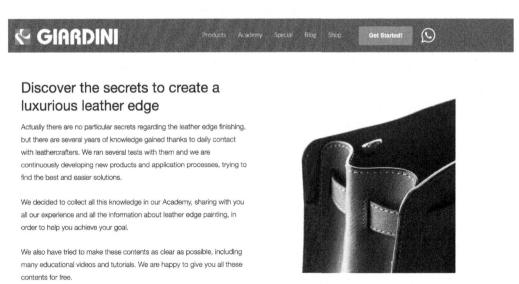

Figure 5G02   From the Giardini's website: the value proposition.

on a small scale all around the world. Probably nobody in the Giardini Group was aware of such a wide production of leather products around the world when Enrico started testing the market.

Turnover hit 300K in the second year, then 450K, 550K, 600K and 800K in 2019, a steady growth that reveals the stable commitment of the company around the marketing project.

Among the reasons why it has been achievable, the very first accomplishment should be attributed to Enrico's entrepreneurial attitude and his clear vision that allowed the company to invest resources in the right actions, facing the decision-making with an awareness of the business mission.

Greatest Challenges Faced

Among the most important efforts Enrico lists are:

- the challenge to define the buyer persona;
- creating contents in a stable, methodical fashion to enable a flow of fresh new ideas on a regular basis;
- staying up to date with tech changes; and
- developing a team.

We wanted to explore what facing those challenges implies.

1. On the "buyer persona" definition, Enrico affirms that it has been an ongoing journey, with errors and U-turns, that has never really ended. Now the definition is pretty much mature; the HubSpot forms the clients fill in on the website contain a question that alone can give a highly accountable ranking of the profile of the buyer and that very question engages them in different conversational sequences, all done by automated email messaging.
2. On "Content Creation," Enrico affirms that it has been the major effort throughout the many company's years in business: it was very hard to find new ideas every day and test them, as you do not know when they will fail or whether they will be able to grab attention. You might work for days on the production of a video that then doesn't get an audience, and then you post a stupid post about something unexpected and it attracts thousands of viewers.

Outcome

Enrico is a positive, proud and happy man; this probably helped him to keep striving. He has no regrets about the efforts he has made, and he feels he would do it again if he were asked to. He now serves in the local community as an elected member of the local administration. Some entrepreneurs have requested Enrico's support during their business development projects. Enrico can tell them the most common errors they should avoid.

On his personal achievement Enrico has been invited to give a speech at The Fashion Institute of Technology in New York.

He only regrets the many errors made: "*...if it was not for the many errors I've done, I could live better, being less stressed and, maybe, achieving more.*"

I couldn't help myself asking: "*Enrico, if you* hadn't *made so many mistakes, would you* have *been able to achieve such awareness?*"

What we can learn

First lesson is for everyone: considering that a small business has been able to achieve this, there are no more excuses for why medium-size companies can't make it as well.

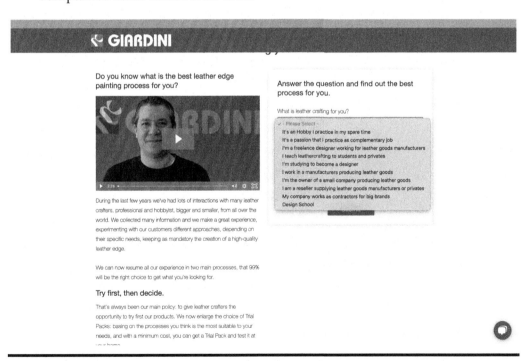

Figure 5G03   Giardini website: the qualification process.

Second lesson: even with digital automation in place, the road to success has no shortcuts.

Third lesson: tools are just tools; we can work better with some of them, but if we do not start from knowing why we want to use them, they won't add much value to our work.

Fourth lesson: they were right, in marketing there is only one P that matters: People.

Chapter 6

Data Architecture

What is the architecture of data? Why and how can a set of fields have an architecture? Are they not all just data?

These are a few questions that often arise during CRM design within organisations. And it is obvious why people wonder about it, as the purpose of the CRM itself is not always clear. To have an understanding of why data need to be organised and planned in quantity, quality and functionality, we need to start with the purpose of CRM. To enable the CRM tool to unfold its full potential we need to design its informative scope.

According to the purpose of creating reporting and deploying information, which is also the final CRM value, we have to decide how wide and deep the information should be, that becomes a parameter to define what and how much data we need. In addition to it we must say that the intrinsic reliability of data implies that we must define how the process of collecting data should be trustworthy. Generally speaking, a trade-off between scope and accuracy is always in place under definite budgets. This is why designing the amount of data required, how the data are to be collected and their hierarchy and contribution to information building is important. And this is what data architecture does.

The topics covered in this chapter are as follows:

1. Information and data
2. Data methodisation
3. Collecting data in real life

DOI: 10.4324/9781003148388-6

Information and Data

A CRM is much more than a data repository. Its purpose is to support business decisions and, in doing that, to smooth the data collection process within the organisation. Hence defining the scope of the information to sustain implies the quantity and the variety of data to be collected, stored and manipulated.

If that concept is easy to understand, controlling the business's desire to dominate everything is less immediately straightforward. The deleterious idea of a client 360-degree view, which has been largely promoted until recent times, has fed companies' appetite for knowing everything about the client, even though it later has been clarified as ineffective.

Business needs information—the more the better. Hence collecting every available datum is the way. Yes, but again, this is the mainstream, wrong approach.

The turning point is:

■ what information each business needs to be effective; and
■ what data take part of that information and how.

These points are the basis for planning efficient and effective data collection. Only by having figured out what we need, then we can better plan the basis to develop it.

We do not deny that the better we can depict the situation of clients, markets, economics, social, political and scientific trends, the better we can design the business strategy. What we believe is that there exists a trade-off between the intent to collect data and the capability of analysing those data at any level. The chimera of taking everything under consideration is almost impossible, and for this reason it can lead to mistakes as well as the lack of information.

> "... *we are, minute by minute, exposed to a monumental amount of data. We simply can't elaborate always, all of them, it would be even highly costly but essentially useless. On the other hand, elaborate data serves us to understand things, their importance, their value.*"*

---

* Testa, A., *Il Coltellino Svizzero*, Garzanti, 2020.

The balance between the effort and the supposed outcome of a wide range of data and information management is what entrepreneurs have to decide.

If corporations can generally rely on a vast amount of resources that enable them in gathering, storing, managing and analyse data and excerpt information, small businesses are often visionless before big sociological and macroeconomic downturns, in fact neither type of company is innocent of wrongdoing. Big corporations fail even if they rely on a much greater amount of qualitative information. Leaving aside the many fraudsters and the robbers,* we consider just errors in reading the environment, markets and technology and how they can be much more common than we are prone to accept. Hence taking decisions that strike the right balance between what we can really control and the effort required is an entrepreneurial skill. And the efficiency and effectiveness of a business strongly rely on that competence.

All this to say that in order to avoid the temptation of gathering too much data—data that later we wouldn't be able to manage, as they can become really confusing—we must focus on what is really important and actually required in terms of information for decision-making processes. By doing that we will be able to better shape the data required and they will probably be a much more manageable amount.

Then in order to define a data architecture for the CRM tool, we have to think of its use, and which processes are under consideration and what data they might require for managing them. The complexity and the kind of sales processes that need to be managed, affect the type of data, in the same way a long-term relationship with the clientele can also impact the type and quantity of data. This is because of the critical role of information required to manage the relationship in an effective way.

We introduced the WHWT model in Chapter 4; let us use it for an example of data gathering. WHWT is about understanding the client's specific situation and needs:

- **W**hat they do
- **H**ow do they do it
- **W**hy they do it
- **T**o whom they do it

---

* Vermeulen, F., *Business exposed: The naked truth about what really goes on in the world of business*, Financial Times, 2012.

Leading information gathering by this simple method can empower the relationship with clients. But these questions lead to qualitative information, not quantitative.

The challenge is to redefine the information in their own basic data to make it manageable.

Let's see an example.

General informative description of a business:

■ They build affordable, high-standard houses.
■ They use modern technologies and efficient approaches to cost reduction.
■ They believe they can enable people to live better under a better cost-effective rate.
■ Their clients are well educated, mainly professionals who appreciate quality and well-being. To these people, the house is not anymore their life's purpose.

Unfortunately, this is just fantasy, but you can now imagine the informative power of this set of information if you run a business focused on builders active in the real estate market. And probably you can also see how to split that information into a dataset.

With a general approach it could be split as follows:

■ Houses
■ High standard
■ Cost effective
■ Medium/high class
■ Well-being
■ Minimalist

Among other notable elements we could include a list of types of technologies adopted. But let's leave that for now.

This is just a very limited and simple example of what it could look like when information is dissected into its components: the data.

Why information about clients and markets is relevant doesn't need to be repeated, but let's consider it a bit more carefully as it leads us to the next stage: under the previous circumstances, what if you run a business that provides components and technologies to building companies?

Knowing this set of information enables you to define what value your solution(s) could provide to that company.

1. If your solutions enable well-being at home and you are capable of providing them in a really cost-effective way, then that company will be very sensitive to your value proposition.
2. If your solutions are high level and you occupy the high price, high standard, high positioning in the market, you will have some possibilities but your high pricing could be a limiting factor.
3. If your positioning in the market is focused on best prices, then you will have limited possibilities to add value to them as long as they stick with the expressed mission.

We can say that this is not something new; it is what every single salesperson or business person knows about each client!

The approach we propose here is to formalise it in terms of data and information. The purpose is to crystallise that data into a dataset, enabling the most useful data collection into a digital CRM that makes the data available at any time as well as making it effective to build the information needed by thus making the information an organisation's asset instead of just a salesperson's personal knowledge. And in doing that, we must consider how to store data to make them searchable and truly able to render information.

The digital CRM should be intended as a productivity booster, enabling faster and better management of a bigger amount of data and being able to utilise them in useful information rendering, so that processes can be run more efficiently.

Let's imagine we want to build an audience of contacts who have certain characteristics, in order to get into communication with them. The creation of queries in the database allows us to shape audiences based on data, not on qualitative information. Consider that qualitative information generally stored as open text allows people to input any kind of words, without any specific structure and with no binding on them. If we stored the general informative description extended as reported before, we would be virtually unable to select this company by any database query. Because it is a free text without any structure that can be selected as data.

Breaking the original extended information down into essential data allows us to create a dataset of consistent elements, such as the same structure of the words, numbers or raw data. This will finally enable data searching.

Let's check with an example. Here are the parameters with their possible patterns:

1. PRODUCTION: Houses / Flats / Villas / Hospitals / Shops / Council houses / ...
2. POSITIONING: High Standard / Luxury / Convenience / Popular / Cost Effective / Lush / Affordable / ...
3. FEATURES: High Class / Middle Class / Executive / Blue collars / Students / Young / ...
4. DISTINCTIVE: Well being / Minimalist / Millennials / Aged / Facilitation

As you can now notice, we reduced the parameters to four and created a dataset of variables that describe each parameter.

The logic of the query is:

Select:

PRODUCTION = Houses
POSITIONING (contains) High Standard (and) Cost Effective
FEATURES (contains) MediumClass (or) HighClass
DISTINCTIVE (contains) Well Being (and) Minimalist

The audience provided will be a list of contacts; they produce Houses, have a market positioning of High Standard with a Cost Effective focus aimed at the middle class or to more affluent clients who care about well-being without showing off.

We can see how the query works; where there are more variables within each selection parameter, the possibility to check for all or at least one of them is the method. For POSITIONING, the query will select contacts that include both "High Standard" and "Cost Effective," while in FEATURES it will select contacts that have "MediumClass" and contacts that have "HighClass." This point is central to query settings and it totally depends on the dataset designed for the database.

If you have those contacts in your digital CRM, you might have just created a list of them. You can address communication using laser-focused messages to engage the specific type of person you wish to target.

This is a multidimensional selection that not only has a more effective use but also enables flexibility. If your business only sells one solution, sold in the same way to the very same buyer persona, you can also create a unidimensional query. Whether you start from the general extended definition or you use the data that you arrived at through segmentation, it would be easy to create one single element: YES/NO. Is it a target? Add: YES. Then select all contacts that have a YES in the field "possible client."

But when the audiences are numerous and they are more complex, you aim for different types of buyer persona, to whom you want to send different messages; then a multidimensional selection enables you to cross parameters in different ways, shaping different target audiences.

Essentially data are elements of information; they are like components, bricks, single portions without any value if taken in isolation. But using them appropriately you can shape a multidimensional body, something that starts to symbolise, to describe something. This is the information, like a wall built by bricks. This has a meaning. When you gather additional information you can shape a more complex matter. This is our idea: a body of information about a topic creates the context, the meaning. When we base our understanding upon one single piece of information—just the wall—we won't be able to see the complexity of the building. It is only when we collect more pieces of information, more walls together, that we begin to see the shape, the structure, we can now outline the building and understand the whole matter a bit more.

Here we started from the information about what the (hypothetical) client does, its whole reason for existing, its own role, values and reason why. We described it along four informative dimensions. Then we broke them down into components—the bricks, the data.

Labour in the opposite direction, building information upon available data, is more common, especially when it is required to develop reporting trends concerning possible clients. Data on a population, collected and analysed in bulk, produce several consistent audiences.

In the CRM, we—should be able—to split data and aggregate them in different ways. Combining data along time and space enables to render structured information about different audiences and trends amid the whole population.

Information technology in the digital era enables the invaluable power of digital marketing on social media that fully leverages the capability of data selection by query and report. Social media platforms own a wide and deep pattern of data on their users; this feature is used for crafting audiences for advertising purposes.

Data Methodisation

There are many ways to organise data into a database. What actually matters here is the inner efficiency of the data structure—the architecture—that provides the best performance for minimal effort.*

In building a digital CRM tool we face the very same challenge: how to design efficient data storage. As this actually seems a tech issue, it is generally undervalued as a business problem. Tech can do almost anything, but the question is about what should be done in keeping with strategic decision making.

Why Data Should Have a Structure

The trap in which many may fall is to build the CRM database along the way, adding a field to store a datum while they see it. This "building as you go" style, we can see, has been introduced to ease the user's control of the system.

DIY and entry-level CRM platforms mainly support this feature, making it a market trend that aims to enable organisations to get control of their systems without excessive dependence on an IT engineer for every little tweak they require. It implies that organisations can save time and money in directly managing the digital tools they use, including the CRM. This opportunity for a more "DIY" approach empowers organisations in many ways even if it also requires a level of know-how that is still not existent or "under development" in many organisations. Nowadays companies are widely adopting digital CRM tools while the world is experiencing a shortage of IT engineers; vendors are stimulating the market, enabling organisations to be more independent from the IT service providers. The result of this is an even stronger boost in the adoption of CRM tools by lowering their overall cost. But it is a process that requires a significant investment in knowledge development, understanding what elements are under the business control and what possibilities are related to the technology applied. Deciding how to break down information into data and how to combine data to render information is a central point. In the previous section we have seen how the function of queries selection works, hence we can also understand how to reshape information upon a population, selecting what we need to use

---

* Stephens, R., *Beginning Database Design Solutions*, Wiley, 2009.

in the query. In doing that we can also see another important task: how to extract the possible interesting audiences from a wider population.

Let's imagine we select a list, like Dun & Bradstreet (D&B) or BoldData. The latter proposes its service as follows:

> *"....also uses the same financial sources as D&B, such as local chambers of commerce and financial statements. But we don't stop there. We add 200+ extra data fields from other sources. This results in higher coverage of websites, email addresses, mobile phone numbers, latitude/longitude, revenue, employee size, opening hours, geocodes, import/export. These sources include chambers of commerce, market surveys, business listings, directories, magazines, public records, websites, conferences, telephone directories, publishers, social media and commercial partnerships. All our data is verified by automated processes and human eyes on an ongoing basis. Our database is about 341.897.577 businesses worldwide."*

Well, here we are in the opposite situation. We do have a set of data, the challenge is to create queries that help us in finding, out of 350 million companies, just a few hundred that will buy our product (!)

The worst idea would probably be to start with 341 million emails or cold calls. The challenge of digging for opportunities can't start with old-fashioned, blunt methods, and the idea of digging out the buyer persona should remain in place.

This amount of data to explore is just an example of the challenge of data management in a CRM. In this case, it is quite simple to decide which parameters to control in order to shrink down the list. The challenge can become more complex when other elements are added to the dataset. Let's say that we select 10,000 companies with some shared characteristics that fit with our production/service. And let's imagine we expect several kinds of buyer persona within that audience, hence we have to profile (see Figure 6.1) them in order to figure out WHWT:

■ What they do
■ How they do what they do
■ Why they do it
■ To whom they do it

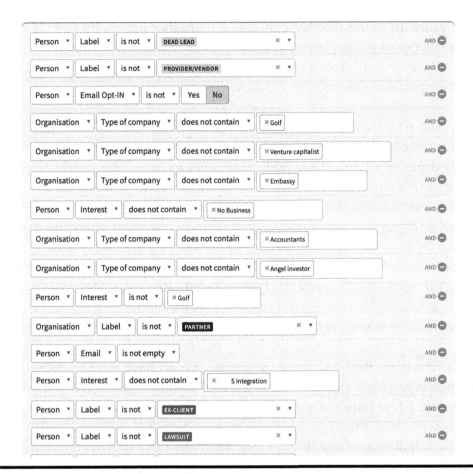

Figure 6.1 An example of a query on many parameters (30).

It means adding more fields to store data. Then we will end up with some very complex queries. That should include many parameters which are searched for different values. When the system is complex, queries of multiple parameters become relevant to select out more focused audiences.

Now everyone can see how important it is to control the content which is allowed to be stored in each field to be able to select the right data and records when creating queries.

Data Optimisation

There are some simple rules that should lead the data architecture design. It is all about constraints; here we can list them:

■ Selection Parameters (data fields) should always be "single choice" or "multiple choice" avoiding free text.

- Constraints should be on numbers and values.
- Constraints should also include phone numbers under the standard E.123.
- Mailbox structure, mostly called "email" or "email address" the mailbox should provide a check on the format of the input, an example is xxxx@xxxx.xxxx where the @ and the dot are the constraints.
- Physical address should be linked to Google Maps and confirmed.

But what is paramount is the control on what each dataset allows for each multiple or single choice. When we get a list of marketing contacts or we integrate or download data from apps, those data are often text or integer. It is our recipient system that should control the data allowed. Let's have a look at a very common and ordinary issue: the phone number. Many systems allow free input. Some include the idea (or more probably lack of a clear idea) that users can also use Skype names there. Well, let's analyse the effect of this decision.

Possible problems:

- Lack of the E.123 standardisation makes it impossible to use VoIP systems.
- Different types of data can create problems in using any phone technology: impossible to link the field content to the phone for a call.
- Different types of data cannot be recognised by integrated apps.
- Often data can go missing: including instructions in the very same field puts things out of control (office, home…, wife's number…).
- Digit errors cannot be checked.

Possible Benefits:

- Fields may be filled easily
- Fields can contains different type of data: it get faster to fill them in
- What else?

A similar pattern of problems can be considered for any kind of data. While the field "Phone Number" is a quite trivial example, so is the field "Address," and everyone can see the risks of leaving those fields open for free text.

Being able to see the risk in theory does not always help to prevent misuse of fields. Many databases and CRM are still weak or lack controls, and they allow users to set the data "as they like," It often seems the simplest and fastest way to enable users to set their own way. Unfortunately people are not used to thinking strategically with data, and the use of free text makes them feel enabled to use the fields for more purposes, avoiding the annoying limitations that constraints imply. The power of a structured dataset is not immediately clear if we do not think strategically. Some questions that help to guide and nurture awareness of the problem could be as follows:

- What information do we want to build using that data?
- How will they be stored?
- Who will input them?
- What queries are we going to create?

A more comprehensive approach might suggest that some limitations that a constraint system in place implies will pay off in terms of efficiency of data management later.

The Kernel of Data Architecture

The essence of Data Architecture is that a lot of data can be treated like the phone number above:

1. Consider the benefits and risks of each option such as using free text or a locked-in selection.
2. If the free text is not beneficial, then plan a pattern of constraints and guidance that limit the input errors and also improve the rendering of more reliable information.
3. Consider the relationship between the datum in that field and its use to define what "shape" the allowed contents can have.

But what really matters for efficient data architecture is the methodology for working with the data pattern as it can be done with an architectural design. Architects design objects that should be beautiful, useful and efficient. *"To build a pillar 2 metres wide I didn't need an architect!"** The concept is simple: make things work within limited resources, efficiently.

In Information Technology, there are no bricks and mortar pillars, but there are many ways to make things unintentionally worse, and when it comes to data it can be easy to lose control of how information is built

---

* Bovio, P., *About the value of an architect*, public speech, 1995.

and upon what data. Essentially losing data can lead to information loss and, eventually, business opportunities losses. In the example at the beginning of this chapter, under "Information and Data," we had six elements taken out of the general extended description. We then included them within four different parameters, with a process of deciding and including descriptive words in one parameter instead of two. This process can be seen as a simplification of the parameters to control: nesting data into a lower number of parameters to better control both their input and output.

When a database contains dozens or even hundreds of data fields, this reduction is not trivial. What can be input and where, for what reason and in which format becomes paramount to controlling the efficiency of the system.

If the labour of extracting an audience in order to analyse a trend is done over dozens of data fields where we can't be sure they have a systematic dataset, the effort required to extract reliable information can be not appropriate for the outcome.

Other approaches can be to create a dataset of six words to store in one data field, or six data fields with one for each dimension, or even as many data fields as possible allowed words. The point is that there isn't one correct solution but the solution should be designed in line with the informative purpose of the data and the needs and importance of the dataset itself.

Data architecture implies thinking in terms of a comprehensive approach: systematic thinking that encompasses sources and output, resources and outcome, behaviour and confidence. Decide what to do in order to control how data affects the expected outputs is the final purpose. Bad outputs due to bad data are more common than they are generally thought.

Collecting Data in Real Life

Effects and Risks

Collecting data to develop a clear, unique and complete view of the audience has been found to be ineffective mainly because of two reasons:

1. Collecting all the possible data is arduous.
2. Even if someone can achieve it, the view developed about a "living being," either a consumer or a company, is just a frame in the movie of life. The very next day it will be something else.

It would be fantastic to know as much as possible about an audience with whom we want to communicate, as we would like to engage all possible prospects. But what would be the marginal value of that dataset compared to the effort required to collect all those data and use them, not to mention keeping them up to date?

What we believe is that there exists a balance between effort and outcome where data are enough to build useful information to make decisions.

As we know, perfect decision-making is a chimera and the process is based on some clear characteristics where deepening data and velocity are inversely related.

Each purpose and scope has different patterns of those two attributes. It is thus the data architect's duty to guide the business in defining the dataset and the quantity and type of data fields to use in accordance with the type and class of data to store.

In real life when people have to deal with data input or data manipulation, the lack of a correct structure of data leads to inefficiencies, wasted time, loss of data and money and, even worse, disheartenment for people.

When salespeople are expected to spend an excessive amount of time gathering data and managing administration duties related to that data, probably something can be changed. Information technology systems that smooth processes and make people work better are great, while digital solutions that are felt as worsening working conditions risk sinking organisations and businesses.

Summary

In this chapter we walk through the obscure matter of data management, something that is clear to data scientists but not so much for business people. Becoming aware of the effects of the data collection process to the business performance can enhance the care for this matter.

■ We highlighted how data and information are related, how the latter develops the former, and how qualitative information strongly depends on the quality of quantitative data.

■ In order to reach efficiency in the data collection we propose a method of collecting data, define a structure of them, pursue their optimisation through a proper design of data architecture.

■ Design the data collection matters in terms of facing the challenge of real life data processing management. Considering how and why errors in data processing can happen explain why we have to create boundaries on it to enhance the quality of data.

Chapter 7

Reporting and Forecasting

We are now able to blend data from different sources and shape trends, figure out the details as well as the overview of the whole population or split it into different audiences. The informative power of a CRM tool includes reporting of processes and sales forecasting. These two decisive tools enable the organisation to pursue control over processes and plan improvements by tracking the effort, checking results and shaping the upcoming trends.

The topics covered in this chapter are as follows:

1. Process Reporting
2. Reporting and Forecasting in B to B, complex sales processes
3. Pipeline Analysis
4. Opportunities Analysis
5. Activities Analysis
6. People Analysis
7. Financial Analysis
8. About Metrics
9. The Survivor Bias
10. Sales Team Surviving Strategy
11. About Today's Reporting
12. What is Expected to be Foreseen
13. Reporting and Forecasting Tool Choice
14. Some possible tools
15. Summary

DOI: 10.4324/9781003148388-7

Process Reporting

Reporting and Forecasting are valuable features for complex processes that manage worthwhile outcomes. High-valuable business processes such as leads generation, sales and customer care are both costly and revenue generating, hence they are worth to be tracked, to plan improvements for and finally measure them. Digitalisation of processes creates the capability of tracking performance and productivity and, on top of that, analysing them and plan for possible improvements. In reality this can be done with almost any digital tool, even Excel spreadsheets, but issues on how to do it and mostly the mismatched balance between the effort required to design and implement a reporting on spreadsheets and its reliability, may dramatically shift this critical activity of reporting into a lack of action. People who can't rely on strong, reliable and steady platforms may allocate time inefficiently by doing that.

Adopting more sharp and comprehensive tools facilitating the setting of those valuable features for the best results and getting reliable information by measuring the effects of any alteration will instead be of paramount importance for any business, hence creating the best tech environment for that is still of primary importance.

We have seen in previous chapters the process of leads generation, sales process and customer care, as well as the way to track activities within them. Here we will list some tips and approaches to Reporting and Forecasting, mainly concerning the sales process as this is the process under more relevant impact of the CRM and ultimately generating revenues.

Reporting on the sales process is relevant not only to improve the efficiency of sales, but also to bolster the effectiveness of the business as a whole. Enhancing efficiency in sales has also the effect of enabling salespeople to work better and be happier about outcomes, and everyone knows how that can improve effectiveness in sales.

Efficient planning and reporting of the sales process implies a reliable and steady data input. This is why we stressed the importance of data architecture settings, as according to the garbage in/garbage out (GIGO) rule, if we want to get sense out of the database, we need to feed it with clean and correct data.

Reporting and Forecasting into B to B, Complex Sales Processes

The decision of *what to report* can be drawn down at the CRM design stage. Of paramount importance is to take into account that technology can enable any kind of data management, thus the problem must be seen as: *what will be useful to know*. This concept stresses the matter of the purpose of information. Knowing what to measure is a business decision, not a technical one.

In a long sales process, it takes time to complete the cycle; this means that each deal can sit for weeks or months in the process, and a lot of things can happen in that time frame as well as decisions being made on the basis of what has been done or not done. But even sales processes of just a few days are worth tracking carefully to improve what is going to happen. Hence reporting becomes vital in planning and controlling when the complexity is high. According to the previous view, organisations should carefully plan the information pattern to boost the informative power of data, something that is not always so straightforward as we might think. As Eric Ries pointed out, defining the trends to measure organisations can fall into the Vanity Metrics* pattern: the tracking of events that are only a little or not at all useful to improve. Different businesses may have completely different metrics that impact on their growth. Even then, generally speaking, we can develop a taxonomy of key performance indicators (KPIs) that are always relevant for sales process performance in business-to-business.

Experts in performance measurement have identified a significant barrier to improved measurement: the need for senior management to agree on the business performance model for their firm before a comprehensive system of performance measurement can be developed.†

Sales process KPIs

- Pipeline: Performance, Sales Cycle Time
- Opportunities: Velocity, Conversion, Value
- Activities: Open, Done in time, Overdue, Done per Deal won, Done per Deal on average, Done per Deal lost

People KPIs

- New Contacts Growth
- MQL growth
- SQL growth
- New Customer Growth

---

* Ries, E., *The Lean Startup*, Crown Publishing, 2011.
† Payne, A., *Handbook of CRM*, Elsevier, 2005.

- ■ Churn Rate
- ■ Nature of audiences
- ■ CS
- ■ SLA compliance

Financials KPIs

- ■ CAC
- ■ Opportunities Profitability
- ■ CLV

The list can be extended according to each business's needs. Let's analyse the function and use of those parameters. As everyone can clearly figure out, the sales process is the centre of the analysis, and contacts as well as financials are also related to it.

Pipeline Analysis

Performance is mainly a measure of effectiveness: the number of deals managed by time period versus the rate of closure per period, that is, input versus output. The more deals are opened, the more deals are going to close, but how this rate changes with time and through quantities is an indicator of the efficiency of the process.

- ■ Adding an X quantity of deals on a sales process that is managing a Y quantity of deals producing a Z number of closures should add a [Z/Y * X) more closure.
- ■ But it can also happen that adding the same quantity of new deals to the same sales process in different periods may produce different outputs.

Sales Cycle Time is the average time from entering in the sales process of each deal and its outcome, either won or lost. The average Sales process Cycle Time and its standard deviation may be a relevant parameter that defines how the sales department works as a whole. Tracking the average time's trend can highlight the financial needs of the business.

Keeping these parameters trend under control may tell us quite a lot about the sales process health and business tendencies.

Opportunities Analysis

Going into details of sales by analysing the journey of opportunities gives more insight into the sales process. This is probably the most common area of analysis and it can be overvalued if it isn't properly balanced by other metrics. This is why multivariate analysis should be taken into account by starting in-depth analysis on these metrics:

- **Velocity** is the speed at which an opportunity moves through each stage of the process, how long it sits in each stage, if it jumps stages or if it is closed before the expected stage. Velocity on average from the point of entering to the closure of the process matches with the Sales Cycle Time, but it is the behaviour between stages that matters here.
- **Conversion** is the trend of opportunities that have been going to closure. A quite obvious parameter as long as we consider closure as the deal being won; slightly less obvious if we want to also track lost opportunities' trend and each reason why they didn't close.
- **Value** of opportunities as a trend and its standard deviation may say quite a lot about the attractiveness of the business with regard to the expected characteristics of clients' requirements.

These parameters make even more sense when analysed in conjunction with variables like:

- type of opportunity
- type of buyer persona
- geographical areas
- products/services involved
- markets served
- and more...

A multivariate analysis will highlight the subtle trends that can empower sales managers to focus on priorities and understand different cohorts of customers.

> *Keeping Velocity and Conversion parameters in control provides insights into the sales process health and its improvement areas, while their variation over time following the sales process changes may unveil market risks and/or opportunities, it may also reveal sales team efficiency trends. The Deal Value trends analysis may reveal either an effect of the brand's attractiveness of the right dimension of opportunities or how markets respond to the brand's positioning journey.*

Activities Analysis

Activities that are done during the sales process matter as they measure the effort of salespeople in running sales. This parameter is not as popular as it deserves to be, even if the Activities Based Selling methodology highlighted it long ago. The idea is to develop awareness on what serves to close a deal in terms of average effort and its standard deviation in order to plan the sales team's capability.

Open: how many activities are open at any time can show how managing sales effort is moving over time.

Done in time: each activity should have a deadline, and the ability to hit the deadline regularly is a parameter of workload and smoothness of the process.

Overdue: if and when activities remain overdue and for how long is a parameter that deserves deeper analysis; its trend should be under evaluation regularly.

Done per deal (average per won/lost): according to the conversion trend, the trend of activities done can unveil subtle information about how deals are managed in relation to the win-loss ratio.

A multivariate analysis with the sales team members, markets, buyer persona type and dimension of deals will help in understanding differences between outperformers and underperformers. Planning team alterations and outputs in revenue is also strongly related to measuring the job.

Trends of activities parameters provide an overview of how sales are managed, the effort they require and the use of resources along the process. The amount of output the sales team is capable of, is directly related to the effort applied in deals management but inversely related to the effort required by each deal.

People Analysis

Audiences of leads, prospects and customers and how they change along the leads generation stage and sales process journey can reveal a lot about the effectiveness of sales, the brand character and the type of buyer persona engaged.

New contacts' growth rate is a parameter of the leads generation stage but can be relevant to grasp the overall attractiveness of the brand, especially when compared with resources invested in marketing or actions on customer retention and satisfaction as they can report their experiences and thereby can influence new clients.

Marketing Qualified Leads growth rate highlights the capability of the marketing effort to engage the right targeted audiences. Especially in organisations that perform qualification of leads after the first engagement, this parameter can help to clarify how many of the interested people entering the funnel are effectively qualified to become a client.

Sales Qualified Leads growth rate works in the same way as the previous one, but this rate can be less dependent on the marketing effort and probably more related to inner trends of markets.

New customers' growth rate is a clear KPI which can be valuable to track over types of customer separately, especially when it comes to recurring clients.

Churn *rate* shows the trend of clients who halt the service or do not buy anything else when they instead could buy more, seeing this way can be relevant to investigate why they don't proceed or they abandon the brand. Ultimately how good the business is perceived by clients.

Nurture of audiences is a metric about communication with different audiences of people, ranging from unknown to established clients. Typical indicators span from number of contacts engaged in communication, to number of contents reshared, number of quotations and referrals. The more the brand awareness grows, the better the brand is perceived and the more contents developed are able to provide value to its audience, the better the audience growth and so do the market opportunities. This is the typical digital marketing area where metrics are well known and sometimes over-considered,* but in terms of a holistic approach to the brand's presence in the markets, they can provide trends that may be useful to keep under control.

Customer Care Cases trend and *Service-Level Agreement* compliance are two KPIs that detect the level of customer engagement and the

---

* Kernan, S., *The campaign that got Taco Bell's CEO fired*, Medium, 2020.

smoothness of the user experience. Customer engagement is a side effect of the user experience; if clients accept to buy notwithstanding imperfections in the usage of the product/service, it may depend on the level of engagement they perceive for the brand: the less the brand is beloved by its clients, the more the complaints can be harsh, and people are less likely to accept low levels of user experience or performance.

> *Analysis on contacts enables the sales process analysis on a different level: the people. Why and how people react or they engage with the brand, what actions impact on trends, how audiences grow and how profitable they are, are just a few questions that facilitate better decision-making.*

Financials Analysis

Reporting on financial performance is an important area and generally very well governed by CFOs. We do not need to go through that area here, but just recall some relevant KPIs more closely related to CRM.

Customer Acquisition Cost is a typical metric of digital marketing, but is a parameter that we all can measure either on and off-line. Generally it is calculated per average cost where the numerator is the marketing investment and the denominator is the number of new clients won. The trend of CAC among its different dimensions for different populations of buyer personas and different channels or media adopted is a pattern of metrics that can tell quite a bit about the effort a brand needs over time and between different channels and different types of customers.

Opportunities profitability is a less easy-to-use parameter when dealing with complex services, much easier instead when dealing with products. This KPI shows the gross profit margin contribution and, by knowing that, decisions can be made on where efficiency could be introduced to extract more value or about how to create more value that clients are keen to pay for.

Client Lifetime Value is a well-known metric, but it is often considered below its possibilities. It remains an extremely relevant parameter when considering the value creation process and the relationship between client acquisition costs and sales process management costs. The limit of this parameter relies on its formation, which may be strongly based on assumptions, something that happens very often in the early stages of the business.

To collect more reliable figures some businesses might have to wait quite a long time, but it is the proper tracking of events and interactions over time that empowers this dimension to unleash its full potential.

> *Financial reporting is nothing new, but what matters here is its close connection with other data extracted within the relationship with clients that empowers multivariate analysis capable of providing important correlations and enabling better business decisions.*

About Metrics

There are two approaches to consider when designing a business reporting system that we care to highlight here. The first is focused on the start-up time, but with some adapting, we believe it can also be relevant for established companies. In fact the learning and innovation process is always in place in healthy businesses.

What Eric Ries formulated is a milestone in measuring business trends, as he included the idea of "innovation accounting" to enable deep analysis of the capability to track what progress an organisation makes along its innovation pathway.

> *"I recently met with a phenomenal startup team. They are well financed, have significant customer traction, and are growing rapidly. Their product is a leader in an emerging category of enterprise software that uses consumer marketing techniques to sell into large companies. For example, they rely on employee-to-employee viral adoption rather than a traditional sales process, which might target the chief information officer or the head of information technology (IT). As a result, they have the opportunity to use cutting-edge experimental techniques as they constantly revise their product. During the meeting, I asked the team a simple question that I make a habit of asking startups whenever we meet: are you making your product better? They always say yes. Then I ask: how do you know? I invariably get this answer: well, we are in engineering and we made a number of changes last month, and our customers seem to like them, and our overall numbers are higher this month. We must be on the right track." ...*

> *"Unfortunately, this is not a good indicator of whether a startup is making progress. How do we know that the changes we've made are related to the results we're seeing? More importantly, how do we know that we are drawing the right lessons from those changes? To answer these kinds of questions, startups have a strong need for a new kind of accounting geared specifically to disruptive innovation. That's what innovation accounting is."**

Eric focuses his approach on start-ups, but we wonder: how much could established companies learn from that?

The second important contribution that Eric Ries developed in his book is the concept of "Vanity Metrics." This concept highlights the importance of focusing on certain, less evident, measurements instead of just measuring what is easy to track. Good metrics are often not immediately clear for managers, where easy metrics are, instead, straightforward to acquire and they often show good trends, but they always mislead business decisions. Relevant metrics are sometimes painful, while vanity metrics aren't:

> *"For a report to be considered actionable, it must demonstrate clear cause and effect. Otherwise, it is a vanity metric. Take the number of hits to a company website. Let's say we have 40,000 hits this month—a new record. What do we need to do to get more hits? Well, that depends. Where are the new hits coming from? Is it from 40,000 new customers or from one guy with an extremely active web browser? Are the hits the result of a new marketing campaign or PR push? What is a hit, anyway? Does each page in the browser count as one hit, or do all the embedded images and multimedia content count as well? Those who have sat in a meeting debating the units of measurement in a report will recognise this problem.*
>
> *Vanity metrics wreak havoc because they prey on a weakness of the human mind. In my experience, when the numbers go up, people think the improvement was caused by their actions, by whatever they were working on at the time. That is why it's so common to have a meeting in which marketing thinks the numbers went up because of a new PR or marketing effort and engineering thinks the better numbers are the result of the new features it added. Finding out what is actually going on is extremely costly, and so most*

---

* Ries, E., *The Lean Startup*, Crown Publishing, 2011.

managers simply move on, doing the best they can to form their own judgment on the basis of their experience and the collective intelligence in the room.

Unfortunately, when the numbers go down, it results in a very different reaction: now it's somebody else's fault. Thus, most team members or departments live in a world where their department is constantly making things better, only to have their hard work sabotaged by other departments that just don't get it. Is it any wonder these departments develop their own distinct language, jargon, culture, and defense mechanisms against the bozos working down the hall?

*Actionable metrics are the antidote to this problem. When cause and effect is clearly understood, people are better able to learn from their actions. Human beings are innately talented learners when given a clear and objective assessment."** *

Another author who has portrayed metrics about CRM in a relevant fashion is Adrian Payne, in his *Handbook of CRM:*[†]

"The identification of appropriate metrics is another challenge for companies seeking to evaluate and enhance their CRM performance. The main problem lies in determining the critical measures of CRM-related activity that are most appropriate to the organisation and managing them effectively. It is important at this stage to note the distinction between metrics and KPIs. Metrics involve all those CRM-related activities that should be measured.

Key performance indicators are the high-level measures that are critical to the success of the business and that should be monitored closely by the Board and top management.

We consider four main categories of CRM metrics are especially important:

- *customer metrics*
- *operational (employee and process) metrics*
- *strategic metrics and output*
- *comparative metrics.*

---

* Ries, E., ibidem.
[†] Payne, A., *Handbook of CRM,* Elsevier, 2005

These key metrics represent the 'vital statistics' of healthy CRM, sig-nalling the strength or weakness of the underlying CRM processes. Other more specialized metrics may also be needed to meet specific company requirements. In any event, these CRM metrics should be applied regularly to provide an overall appraisal and monitoring of CRM effectiveness.' *

The concept of what to measure in order to shape information that is truly useful to decision-makers is a relevant theme. The logic of CRM can lead to the understanding of what is relevant for the clients; meanwhile CRM as a tool enables that. Adrian's contribution clarifies how complex is the choice of metrics to design effective reporting. While not all metrics are useful, some are specifically relevant at operational levels and others have impact at the strategic level.

What Eric Ries reported was a learning process upon which they were educated to measure and what they discovered was painfully relevant for their business survival. Eric says: *"When numbers go up, everyone is ready to take accountability of that, when numbers go down it is always someone else's responsibility."* And it was when numbers went badly down that Eric Ries's team had to discover how to measure where they were and what direction they should follow.

Quantitative versus Qualitative Information Reporting

Reporting is often expected to be a comprehensive tool able to tell the story of the content: numbers do not talk, explanations are required to be added on top of them. For instance, a company's profit and loss sheet reports num-bers and qualitative explanations of decisions taken or recommendations that serve to guide the understanding of trends and results.

Well, this is an interesting point about reporting that should be high-lighted properly: automated reporting on data is not yet featured by AI to develop automated clarification of trends and meaning over data tendencies.

There is the possibility that someone will develop it soon, but we would wonder about the benefit of a feature like that. Hence when qualitative reporting is expected, we suggest designing business processes where automations provide the analytics of the data and, using that, humans can

---

* Payne, A., *Handbook of CRM*, ibidem.

thereafter develop the qualitative information that would be useful for decision-making.

At the moment, expecting an automated procedure to add qualitative information is something that would require a lot of effort for a probably limited value delivered.

The Survivor Bias

The last point about reporting is a warning about what we have to watch: what we are tempted to analyse is not always what helps us to improve.

> *"The US army inadvertently bumped into survivorship bias when they considered how to reduce airplane losses during WWII under enemy's fire. Examining the airplanes' damage they decided to add armor to the most damaged areas that logically were the most hit by enemy bullets.*
>
> *Abraham Wald at the Statistical Research Group at Columbia University contradicted the US military's conclusions. Wald noted the military only considered the aircraft that had survived their missions; any bombers that had been shot down or otherwise lost had logically also been rendered unavailable for assessment. The bullet holes in the returning aircraft, then, represented areas where a bomber could take damage and still fly well enough to return safely to base. Thus, Wald proposed to reinforce areas where the returning aircraft were unscathed, as those were the areas that, when hit, would cause the plane to fall."**

This small story tells us that in order to improve something we need to focus on more complex and, sometimes, sorrowful metrics: it is great to celebrate successes and they can teach us quite a lot when properly analysed, but what we can learn in more depth is from the analysis of reasons of explicit failure, which can sometimes be even more relevant to avoid the same issues again and find new ways to improve.

---

* Wald, A., *A method of estimating plane vulnerability based on damage of survivors.* Statistical Research Group, Columbia University, 1943 [https://apps.dtic.mil/dtic/tr/fulltext/u2/a091073.pdf].

Sales Team Surviving Strategies

If this approach is absolutely crystal clear and well known in the management community, what is less clear is what holds organisations in the survivor bias, at least in sales. What we believe is that the sales role is quite different from other roles in the organisation; the salespeople have the responsibility of money generation, their capability impacts on the clients' engagement, on the income and ultimately on the business success. Organisations are more keen to accept mistakes when it comes to product's development or project management; while mistakes in sales are too often considered a lack of salespeople capability, even because they have a direct impact on the income generation. Mistakes in sales happen no matter if the product is absolutely fine and the marketing is correct, hence they really burns opportunities that were there ready to be yielded!

A mistake of a salesperson is often blamed for diminishing all the good that has been done to prepare the sales. We all have heard statements like these: *"Once we have done* everything *right, salespeople haven't been able to convert,"* or even *"Our problem is on sales, if we only* had *capable salespeople …".*

Of course salespeople may often be not capable, they often fail, they might lack core competencies. Oddly enough they do this exactly as much as everyone else does. But they are responsible for directly generated income and this is a burden that no other role of the organisation takes on its shoulders. Hence it is easy to overvalue salespeople and celebrate them when they win and even easier to blame them when they don't.

Then, of course, organisations complain they can't find good salespeople, but great organisations invest in salespeople to grow their competencies, creating environments where they are able to track their own effort, their own achievements and their own failures in the confidence that mistakes are unavoidable for everybody, and a learning process for this organisation's role also includes, painfully, income losses.

Furthermore, and because of that responsibility, salespeople are not often keen to discuss or analyse their failures. Very probably as nobody else really enjoys it either, they are not the first who will dig out the missing point of what they have done. Especially when they operate within an organisation that is not keen to track "innovation accounting," the learning-by-mistakes process that Eric Ries introduced.

What, instead, becomes the mainstream is to keep measuring what is going well, for them but eventually bad for others: number of leads-in for instance, taking for granted that the conversion rate is stable, the focus has to be shifted on the need to receive more fresh, well qualified leads? The customer experience appraisal can be another example; is it the constant rate of reported bad experience due to the product's low performance or to customer's expectations setting during the sales process?

These are only two examples of many possible questions that consultants often place over the business processes as a whole. Not blaming anyone.

In reality, to be able to face our own failures and mistakes we all need to feel comfortable, and accepting the mistakes of anyone in the organisation is a basic setting to make people feel comfortable. Where organisations take on board methods like the Celebration Grid* also in the sales team management, then the organisation's capability of facing failures improves. Mistakes are seen as an unavoidable part of the process and the focus is placed on the need to measure correct metrics than develop adjustments at any level, accounting it as a learning process to hit better outcomes. Not just survive the storm, avoiding responsibility, but engaging with positive improvements for the whole organisation.

The CRM is the tool that may support organisations to enable those kinds of positive environments. The ability to focus on errors as well as successes, to dig out information on what hasn't worked in prospects that didn't convert (which are always the majority) is the essence of improvement in sales and management.

Reporting is the CRM feature which strongly supports that, and to achieve it there are no shortcuts but only a focused journey to experiment and learn what works.

About Today's Reporting

Reporting in business is a vital duty, nothing new. What is still happening in many companies is that they perform it using Enterprise Resource Planning systems. Which is fine as long as they reach their goals. What may be relevant is to clarify that ERP has different purposes from CRM. They can share some data, but what is useful on the ERP sometimes doesn't really matter for the CRM purpose; most importantly, what *does* matter for the CRM is not really useful for the ERP purpose. They have two approaches to business management that go in pairs but are not the same.

To clarify it, let's analyse the two acronyms:

Enterprise Resource Planning
The focus is on resources involved in the business processes. ERP enables analysis of processes upon employed resources to highlight the value created by the whole business process.

---

* Appelo, J., *Management 3.0*, Pearson Ed., 2011.

Customer Relationship Management

The focus of the CRM as a tool is to support the process of nurturing the interdependence with the market through company's stakeholders relationships, namely the ones that are, have been or can be clients, supporting better connections and more clear comprehension of trends and feelings.

We can see that the two uses of them involve different datasets.

To make it simple let's say that:

- in the ERP we track the output, and how we create it using available resources, then eventually resources received in exchange of it
- in the CRM we track how we interact with the counterpart of the business, the people who receive our production, then eventually how they behave, what they choose and why they like us.

This is the reason why ERP is not enough for reporting other than financials and absolutely not useful for forecasting when it is not based only on the projection of the past into the future.

Let's clarify that the CRM tool may create better projection of future opportunities when used in B2B business models with complex and long sales processes. When the sales process is short and/or the clients are consumers the CRM tool may mainly contribute with past trends analysis: moods, feelings and behaviours tracked that may also provide a support to a better analysis.

In the end, CRM tools can help R&F in different ways in line with the business needs, style and ways to make business. That's why today the decisions on adopting CRM tools are now largely mainstream around companies all over the world. The matter is not whether or not to implement a CRM, but what tool would be right. We would like to contribute to the public discussion by moving the debate beyond the tech tool. Organisations that implement the tool should proceed from the logic they want to pursue. We will discuss it later, but it is important to set it as the foundation of further considerations.

Forecasting on Sales Process

*"Sales Teams Aren't Great at Forecasting: Here's How to Fix That."** The title of the *Harvard Business Review* article by Bob Suh, published in March 2019, didn't leave much to guess. But Bob doesn't place full responsibility on

---

* Suh, B., *Sales teams aren't great at forecasting. Here's how to fix that*, HBR, 2019.

salespeople; his contribution actually takes account of the human nature to whom we all are submitted. What is absolutely important is to know that, and design environments and systems that allow people to get benefits of more reliable behaviours aim to reduce personal accountancy for the good as well as for the worse and ultimately keep control of any possible and always easy to adopt, opportunistic behaviours.

Bob ends his article with a clear warning: *"More accurate predictions of sales are important for individual businesses and for our economy. If we do encounter more volatility, forecasts which have historically been inflated by 8% could soon be off by as much as 20 to 50%. Leaders owe their shareholders a better method of predicting revenues."*

Forecasting, more than reporting, has an extremely critical function for any organisation:

> *"When I arrived to be promoted to sales director, I was proud of my career, I went around to talk to different people in different roles in the organisation and everyone was keen to support me. Then the board asked me my plan and forecast for the year coming revenue. I went down to the organisation asking everyone their budget, and everyone asked me how many of each product we are expected to sell. Anxious and distressed, I went back to my office: everyone's budget depends on the sales forecast, but to whom I could ask for sales prediction wasn't clear. It was a guessing game, speculation about the unpredictable as I didn't have a clue of what the client would have bought the very next year..."*[*]

Not only the company production's plans and the sales team's evolution depend on sales forecasting. Also, economic performance and financial needs rely on sales forecasting and, among financials, capital investors also look at sales forecasting with care.

Saying that, we have set up the basis to discuss what forecasting into CRM tools aimed at sales process management is, and before listing some possible tools that can empower R&F into any type of CRM, let's have a look at methods and know-how that can be useful to rely on at the design stage to enable better forecasting later.

Designing Data Architecture is paramount to prevent data input issues. The more data are standardised, the clearer is input and thus the better any kind of analysis later developed. Improvement of outputs definitely

---

[*] Specchia, A., *Interview to sales directors*, 2003.

relies on a controlled and well-planned data input. When datasets are designed properly, developing analysis will be possible using many options and different Business Intelligence tools; by contrast, when datasets are inaccurately designed, input gets affected by uncertainty, there is lack of clarity on the data pattern or content of each field, and thus the data analysis becomes more complex to develop and any prediction of future revenue will be less reliable.

Designing the information required to feed decision-makers. Information is developed upon data and it is all about the intelligence of data trends and aggregated meaning. Have a clear understanding of what kinds of information aid in developing reliable predictions of the future. The focus should be on the flow from the data, the basic bricks, and how they will compose the wall of information, and how that information should support the rendering of an overarching comprehension of the situation, the building, around us.

Decision-makers are the recipients of information. Design the information building process about forecasting, having in mind who the recipient will be, who would benefit from the information we are going to develop and how they will better understand them. Whenever we create a message we are already used to shaping it according to the recipient's perception. This is even more necessary when recipients have limited time available and strategic decision-making to accomplish. Hence, information has to be concise, direct to the point, and being able to create value using the informative power of the best possible tools becomes a must, not a choice.

Time is a vital factor. We all know that accuracy of information is an essential feature, without which the value of information decreases. But today's challenge is more to rely on real-time information than exact data. The final goal would probably be to gather the most accurate information in less time, possibly with zero delays and 100% accuracy. But the correct balance can often be slightly suboptimal, hence organisations should design their own balance dynamically: planning how much effort to deploy on improving the development of accurate information and how much effort to improve the matching of expected time for decision-making. The subtle value lies in the improvement process.

What Is Expected to Be Foreseen

About this topic we will limit the discussion to what everyone knows about forecasting: the process of seeing (something) fore, to see something before it happens. What would be useful to know about the future for a business? Nothing more than how many people (or businesses) around it will become paying customers and how much customers will pay. Not much really, is it? If only it was so simple we all would be rich by now.

The reality is that to make conjectures about it may require lots of elements and some of them can be only guessed: *"The real challenge in crafting strategy lies in detecting the subtle discontinuities that may undermine a business in the future. And for that there is no technique, no program, just a sharp mind in touch with the situation."* *

More than 30 years ago Henry Mintzberg highlighted the importance of human business acumen in depicting the future. He was right, and even if at that time information technology was almost in its Stone Age compared to today, his thought's contribution remains relevant to this day. But we shouldn't take it wrong: great minds, great leaders are the ones who stay informed every second; they eat information, data, opinions, outlooks, feelings, as any form of available perspective. They watch macro and micro trends, relentlessly. They are the *"...sharp minds in touch with the situation."*

Sales reports are so vital. Well beyond revenue projecting, sales trends are part of the strategy development process. Even if most of the time they remain at the operational level or they are taken with care, the view of the sales department is always an element that supports long-term decisions. Hence organisations are in need of better forecasting; when talking about CRM, the role of this tool becomes cardinal.

In B to B markets with long, complex sales processes, the forecasting can be based on opportunities going to close as per (a) timing, (b) expected value and (c) probability.

Reporting and Forecasting Tools Choice

Some CRM platforms offer integrated features to cover this area while many others don't. This is the domain of business intelligence tools where CRM vendors offer some capabilities related to their tool and based on their own perspective. Even if the trend shows that many CRM tools try to include reporting features as part of their value proposition, quite often those features have limited capabilities. When organisations need to improve their

---

* Mintzberg, E., *Crafting strategy*, HBR, 1987.

analysis performance, the way is to adopt specific Business Intelligence tools.

Here we will list only a few of the most common tools for BI connected to CRM, on a limited but considerate inventory. It would be clearly impossible to list even an acceptable fraction of the 2000+ BI solutions available in the market. We strongly suggest that any organisation investigates the market deeply before committing to any vendor. Too many proposals with different approaches and pricing may really be confusing. The good thing about markets with many competitors is that clients may find a solution that fits their needs even if it will also be a long and tedious selection process. One typical error companies make when approaching solution finding is to consider the different solutions much more similar than what they really are. A realistic consideration shows important differences that should be carefully evaluated before starting to use any solution.

It is also important to know that many solutions can also be easily substituted. The tech issue in substituting a BI tool is not relevant; it will mainly affect users who will be required to face a learning effort. Let's see two foundation methods to guide the selection of tools.

Starting small, thinking big: it is always a great piece of advice. It is easy to commit to expensive tools that promise to take your business to the next level. Then someone has to make it happen. Lean methodology has taught managers to start with minimal resources, testing them and improving them once the learning is achieved.

But 'minimal' is not a unique dimension, any organisation should develop an idea of what is minimal to them. A one-man-band-company can have limited resources (but also very limited benefit) to invest in R&F, while middle-sized enterprises not only can manage more resources, but they need, and deserve, tools that enable them to produce a remarkable outcome. The critical level of their decision-making necessitates the use of reliable, powerful tools. But even for this approach, the cost of different solutions may vary significantly.

What has been observed is that managers who make considerable investments in the early stage of the business do not always get that value back. Management that tests scalable solutions learns how to benefit from them faster; then improving them and eventually changing them is a process that not only enables management to reach a better ROI, but it also nurtures the learning process in teams, so that the whole outcome of the R&F project may improve.

Starting with the final output in mind: BI tools can be very flexible to support data mining in many different databases, but some are less developed than others on the data rendering. Some are better than others at creating complex analyses on many parameters and some others are easier to set up. Everything depends on the purpose the company needs to achieve in terms of reports. It must be taken under consideration that if the tool has lean capabilities, the rendering of data trends could reach a limited informative power. Hence the support of decision-makers would be weaker. Clarifying what is expected and why is one of the parameters for deciding the tool features and performance.

Some Possible Tools

Tableau

Probably one of the most relevant BI platforms that is (almost) ready to use, flexible and powerful for medium-size enterprises. It requires a specialist with a sharp knowledge of the tool and a clear understanding of the organisational requirements. Its pricing is within the market average.

As Gartner Magic Quadrant reports:

It offers a visual-based exploration experience that enables business users to access, prepare, analyse and present findings in their data. It has powerful marketing and expanded enterprise product capabilities, but the integration of Salesforce Einstein Analytics, now renamed Tableau CRM, remains a work in progress.

In 2020, Tableau enhanced its data preparation and data management capabilities. For data preparation, it released enhanced data modelling capabilities, which make it easier to analyse data across multiple tables at different levels of detail by building relationships between tables with a simple in-browser visual experience. For data management, Tableau Prep Conductor and Tableau Catalog offer a cohesive experience for operating and automating data management and understanding data lineage. An Einstein Discovery dashboard extension, the first integrated product to bring the predictive modelling capabilities of Salesforce Einstein Analytics to the Tableau platform, is scheduled for release in March 2021.

Strengths

- *Analytics user experience: although Tableau keeps adding new capabilities, it always maintains a sleek experience for users, so they can perform analysis seamlessly. Although visual-based exploration is highly commoditized in today's market, Tableau can still differentiate itself by offering an intuitive analytics experience with richer capabilities based on its patented VizQL engine.*

■ *Customer enthusiasm: many customers demonstrate a fan-like attitude towards Tableau, as evidenced by the more than 145,000 people who attended its 2020 online user conference. Tableau Public, a free platform on which to publicly share and explore data visualizations online, has over 3 million interactive visualizations. A user-experience-focused design means that, particularly for users in analyst roles, Tableau's offering is compelling and even enjoyable to use.*

■ *Salesforce opportunity: the Tableau Viz Lightning web component offers a low-code experience to simplify the task of integrating Tableau visualizations into Salesforce. Work.com, Salesforce's cloud offering to help organizations reopen workplaces safely and efficiently, uses the Tableau Viz Lightning web component to add a global COVID-19 tracker dashboard to the Workplace Command Center. The deeper integration of the MuleSoft data connector capabilities and a newly acquired Slack collaboration tool means that Salesforce clients have a strengthening set of reasons to consider Tableau.*

Cautions

■ *Not cloud-native: Tableau offers cloud-hosted solutions (Tableau Online and Tableau CRM), but the company's heritage is in on-premises deployments, for which it has a massive installed base. Tableau does not have a cloud-native architecture for on-premises customers to embrace the cloud's full benefits. Deployment of Tableau Server in a containerized infrastructure is not currently supported (but is planned for 2021). As such, beyond Tableau Online, it cannot utilize the cloud's elasticity to automatically scale out in order to handle dynamic workloads.*

■ *Premium pricing: Tableau's pricing is an issue raised by users of Gartner's client enquiry service. Compared with some of the cloud vendors in this market, Tableau is expensive. The addition of Tableau CRM for a list price of up to $150 per user per month may well increase the concern of customers who are considering scaling their deployments or acquiring new functions.*

■ *Integration challenges: as is to be expected, the integration of Salesforce's ABI capabilities with those of Tableau is taking time. Currently, users face a fragmented experience if they want to take advantage of the augmented analytics functions of the former Einstein Analytics while using* *the Tableau platform. Einstein Analytics' strengths in automated data stories, key driver analysis, custom automation and explainable AI are not yet integrated into the Tableau user experience.**

Power BI

Probably the most interesting tool ever made by the company based in Seattle. Its full capability outperforms the needs of a medium enterprise. But in the single-user tier it is a low-cost tool. It requires a well-trained specialist.

It has massive market reach through Microsoft Office and a comprehensive and visionary product roadmap.

Microsoft offers data preparation, visual-based data discovery, interactive dashboards and augmented analytics in Power BI. This is available as a SaaS option running in the Azure cloud or as an on-premises option in Power BI Report Server. Power BI Desktop can be used as a stand-alone, free personal analysis tool. Installation of Power BI Desktop is required when power users are authoring complex data mash-ups involving on-premises data sources.

Microsoft releases a weekly update to its cloud-based Power BI service, which gained hundreds of features in 2020. Notable additions include more augmented analytics in the form of AI-infused experiences, including smart narratives (NLG) and anomaly detection capabilities for out-of-the-box visuals.

Strengths

- *Alignment with Office 365 and Teams: the inclusion of Power BI in the Office 365 E5 SKU has provided an enormous channel for the platform's spread, making it "self-seeding" in many organizations. The increasing integration of Power BI into Microsoft Teams, with its tens of millions of daily active users, will further increase Power BI's reach in the world of remote working. Power BI is now often the option that organizations have in mind when using Gartner's client enquiry service to ask about ABI platform selection—"why not Power BI?" is effectively the question most are asking.*
- *Price–power combination: the influence of Power BI has drastically reduced the price of tools in the ABI platform market since its launch. In*

---

* Gartner, *Magic Quadrant for Analytics and Business Intelligence Platforms*, 2021.

this case, though, low price does not equate to limited functionality. The Power BI cloud service is extremely rich in its capabilities, which include an enlarged set of augmented analytics and automated ML capabilities. AI-powered services, such as text, sentiment and image analytics, are available within Power BI Premium and draw on Azure capabilities.

■ *Scope of product ambition: Microsoft continues to invest in a broad set of visionary capabilities and to integrate them with Power BI. It now claims to have 80,000 customers using AI services in Power BI deployments. It continues to encourage usage at scale by, for example, applying ML-driven automatic optimization of materialized views on Azure Synapse (and soon other data sources, including Snowflake and Redshift) to autotune query performance.*

Cautions

■ *Functional gaps in on-premises version: compared with the Power BI cloud service, Microsoft's on-premises offering has significant functional gaps, including in relation to dashboards, streaming analytics, pre-built content, natural language question and answer, augmentation (what Microsoft calls Quick Insights) and alerting. None of these functions are supported in Power BI Report Server, its on-premises offering.*

■ *Azure only: Microsoft does not give customers the flexibility to choose a cloud IaaS offering. Its Power BI service runs only in Azure. However, customers that utilize Azure can take advantage of the global reach offered by Microsoft's cloud platform. Power BI Premium enables customers to enable multi-geography capabilities in their Power BI tenant, and they can deploy their capacity to one of 42 globally available data centers.*

■ *Content promotion and publication process: the way in which Power BI handles the promotion and publication of content can lead to a significant administrative overhead for customers. The fact that there is a one-to-one relationship between published Power BI apps and Workspaces (Power BI's collaborative "development" environment) means that organizations may face a situation in which they are manually managing many hundreds of Workspaces. Retroactively fixing this issue is a complex task. How to govern self-service usage is perhaps the most common question asked about Power BI by users of Gartner's enquiry service. The Power BI team is, however, investing in governance capabilities to help customers manage their Power BI environments better.**

---

* Gartner, *Magic Quadrant for Analytics and Business Intelligence Platforms,* 2021.

SAS

Probably the most relevant player in the BI arena. It is considered like the Ferrari of the BI domain.

SAS offers SAS Visual Analytics on its cloud-ready and microservices-based platform, SAS Viya. SAS Visual Analytics is one component of SAS's end-to-end visual and augmented data preparation, ABI, data science, ML and AI solution. SAS's extensive Viya-based industry, forecasting, text analytics, intelligent decisioning, edge analytics and risk management solutions use SAS Visual Analytics on Viya.

In 2020, SAS introduced a unique market capability for report reviewing that analyzes reports and suggests good visual design, performance and accessibility practices. It also released SAS Conversation Designer (included with SAS Visual Analytics) for building customized chatbots through a low/no-code visual interface. From a go-to-market perspective, SAS and Microsoft formed a technology and go-to-market partnership, with Azure becoming a cloud provider for SAS Cloud and plans for future SAS integration with Microsoft's cloud portfolio. SAS also introduced new competitive, revenue-capped pricing for SAS Visual Analytics.

Strengths

- *End-to-end platform vision: SAS offers a compelling product vision for customers to prepare their data, analyze it visually, and build, operationalize and manage data science, ML and AI models in a single, integrated visual and augmented design experience (with progressive licensing). Moreover, with Visual Analytics, SAS is the only vendor in this Magic Quadrant to support text analytics natively in a core product.*
- *Augmented analytics: SAS is investing heavily in infusing augmented analytics across its entire platform. This includes investment in automated suggestions for relevant factors, and in insights and related measures and forecasts expressed using visualizations and natural language explanations. Automated predictions with key drivers and "what if?" analysis are supported in SAS Visual Analytics. The platform also features AI-driven data preparation suggestions, voice integration with user devices, chatbot integration and NLG capabilities developed by SAS, rather than an OEM.*
- *Global reach with industry solutions: SAS is one of the largest privately held software vendors, with a physical presence in 47 countries and a*

global ecosystem of system integrators. SAS Visual Analytics forms the foundation for most of SAS's extensive portfolio of industry solutions, which includes pre-defined content, models and workflows.

Cautions

- *Market perception as outmoded: although SAS now supports the open-source data science and ML ecosystem and has introduced a new SDK for SAS Visual Analytics, there remains a perception that SAS is expensive and proprietary. This perception has obstructed consideration of SAS in this market, beyond SAS's installed base. It also impacts the number of new data science and machine learning students that choose to learn SAS, as most focus their studies on open-source platforms.*
- *Inflexibility at contract renewal: despite new capability-based and metered pricing options introduced in 2019, and new, attractive pricing of SAS Viya in 2020, most SAS customers are on older contracts. Gartner enquiries suggest that these customers often perceive SAS contracts as being high-cost and inflexible and as involving difficult renewal negotiations.*
- *Migration challenges: SAS Viya provided a new open architecture and brought modernization to SAS 9 customers, and it is still evolving. However, although SAS has continued to improve its utilities to make migration from earlier releases easier, Gartner enquiries suggest that customers continue to view migration as a challenging undertaking.**

Qlik

It offers augmented ABI functionality fully integrated within the SAP enterprise application ecosystem.

SAP Analytics Cloud is a cloud-native multi-tenant platform with a broad set of analytic capabilities. Most companies that choose SAP Analytics Cloud already use SAP business applications. SAP Analytics Cloud offers an add-in for Microsoft Office 365 on-premises or in the cloud.

In 2020, SAP enhanced its automated insights capabilities by adding new "How has it changed?" and "How is it calculated?" explanation functionality. Also, it rearchitected the self-service user experience workflow to apply augmentation across the data-to-visualization process. Finally, enterprise

---

* Gartner, *Magic Quadrant for Analytics and Business Intelligence Platforms,* 2021.

reporting was updated to add scheduled publication of data stories or PDFs, although it has not achieved parity with SAP BusinessObjects' capabilities in this area.

Strengths

- *Unmatched SAP connectivity: SAP Analytics Cloud is primarily of interest to organizations that use SAP enterprise applications. Seamless connectivity to those solutions is therefore of critical importance. SAP Analytics Cloud has native connectivity to SAP S/4HANA and is embedded in SAP cloud applications, including SuccessFactors and Ariba. Further, despite being cloud-only, SAP Analytics Cloud connects directly to on-premises SAP resources (SAP BusinessObjects Universes, SAP Business Warehouse and SAP HANA) for live data, with no data replication required. Direct data connectivity to non-SAP sources still lags behind that of competitors, however.*
- *Differentiated augmented, closed-loop capability: SAP Analytics Cloud's integrated functionality for planning, analysis and prediction differentiates it from almost all competing platforms. Its ability to conduct "what if?" analysis is combined in SAP Analytics Cloud with a strong, multi-year focus on augmented analytics as a core design tenet. SAP Analytics Cloud offers strong functionality for NLG, NLP and automated insights.*
- *Breadth of capability and content: SAP Analytics Cloud is part of a wider data portfolio that includes SAP Data Warehouse Cloud. SAP Analytics Cloud offers a library of pre-built content that is available online. This content covers a range of industries and line-of-business functions. It includes data models, data stories and visualisations, templates for SAP Digital Boardroom agendas, and guidance on using SAP data sources.*

Cautions

- *Lack of large community: SAP's platform has less market momentum than the ABI platforms of some similarly sized vendors. Judging from public job postings, few organizations are looking to hire staff with skills in, or familiarity with, SAP Analytics Cloud, which is surprising, given the size of the BI installed base that SAP could cross-sell to. This means there is a relatively small user community for SAP Analytics Cloud, at a time when community size is a key driver for selection and adoption because technologies are only marginally differentiated.*

■ *Perception by potential users: Given its BusinessObjects heritage, SAP has been associated with report-centric BI, and the legacy of this is a perception among potential users that does not reflect SAP Analytics Cloud's modern, self-service capabilities. The need to convince potential users that SAP Analytics Cloud is worth considering puts SAP at a disadvantage to the competition in selection processes.*

■ *Cloud-only offering: SAP Analytics Cloud is cloud-native and not available on-premises (although it can query on-premises data). It runs in SAP data centers or public clouds (on AWS and Alibaba, with support for Microsoft Azure planned). It is currently available on data centers in China, Japan, Saudi Arabia, Singapore, United Arab Emirates, Europe, the United States, Canada, Australia and Brazil. For organizations that want to deploy an ABI platform on-premises, SAP's answer is to offer the SAP BusinessObjects BI platform.**

Sisense

Sisense provides an end-to-end analytics platform that supports complex data projects by offering data preparation and visual exploration capabilities and augmented analytics. Over half of Sisense's ABI platform customers use the product in an OEM form.

Sisense 8.2 was released in September 2020 with NLQ capabilities powered by a knowledge graph and Sisense Notebook, which provides code-first augmented Insights.

Strengths

■ *Composable architecture: Sisense has a microservices-based architecture that is fully extensible. Sisense is commonly used to embed analytics capabilities such as interactive visualization and NLQ within a composed analytic application experience to enable better decision-making.*

■ *Comprehensive product capability: Sisense's platform is functionally comprehensive, enabling both business users and expert developers with different skill levels. Cloud and NLQ capabilities are particular strengths.*

■ *Open platform: Sisense is cloud-agnostic and multi-cloud-capable. It has deep partnerships with AWS, Google (GCP) and Microsoft, along with*

---

* Gartner, *Magic Quadrant for Analytics and Business Intelligence Platforms*, 2021.

*strong cross-cloud analytics orchestration. A robust cataloguing capa-
bility supports other analytics vendor assets via APIs. Sisense also offers
extensible connectivity to other reporting tools. An analytics marketplace
in which to publish and build third-party analytics capability is on
Sisense's roadmap.*

Cautions

- *Lower market momentum outside core use case: Sisense has built a successful OEM business with its strong partner programme. This helps it
avoid direct competition with Microsoft (Power BI) and Tableau, which
are dominant in self-service analytics use cases. However, this strategy
means it has less momentum in the wider ABI market. Organizations
choosing Sisense for non-embedded use may, therefore, need to work
hard to present its platform to their user communities as an attractive
alternative to better-known platforms.*
- *Product packaging complexity: Sisense offers a broad set of capabilities, but in three different product packages: Sisense for Product
Teams, Sisense for Cloud Data Teams, and Sisense for Business
Intelligence and Analytics Teams. While indicating the width of
Sisense's overall offering, this approach entails complexity for organizations considering the vendor. Sisense plans to simplify its product
packaging in 2021.*
- *Less consumer-focused: Sisense's new knowledge-graph-enabled NLQ
feature offers new consumer capability, but the platform is generally
focused more on the development ecosystem and personas. Sisense for
Product Teams, an API-first platform, is its best selling product. A new
Sisense DevX Portal is intended to empower developers to build analytics
applications. This vision aligns with Sisense's overall OEM strategy but
may not resonate with potential adopters looking to address the needs of
ABI consumers first.**

Jupyter

This is a data-scientist-only, open-source freeware tool. What makes this
different from any other tool is its capability to support notebook page
creation. Beyond just dashboards with charts, Jupyter Notebook pages can
include qualitative information and charts with real-time data. Imagine you

---

* Gartner, *Magic Quadrant for Analytics and Business Intelligence Platforms*, 2021.

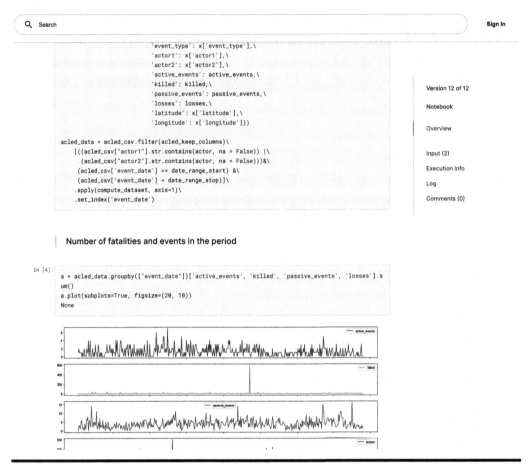

Figure 7.1   A notebook page from Jupyter.

need to prepare a paper on some relevant trends or forecastings where you have to share concepts, reasons why, postulations and you need to put all of them in a document that includes data, charts and graphs using real-time data to support the outcome of analysis.

Jupyter's notebook pages allow you to keep the charts and data connected to your data sources and show powerful data trends in real time (see Figure 7.1).

Summary

The BI area is a valuable market as it is perceived to be relevant for businesses. It has been estimated that more than 2.000 vendors operate in the market. It means that it can really be difficult to choose the right solution at the right price, not because it doesn't exist, but rather because it is hard to evaluate even a small portion of all of them and find the proposals which fit better to your specific requirements. In this situation, big players may have the great advantage on the brand: to avoid risks, managers just go to a handful of big names.

We also listed just a few of them, probably the most known. Actually, there are a plethora of vendors out there; sometimes very small companies are capable of offering pretty interesting solutions aimed to solve some specific problems. If your need is about an engaging rendering of some trends to be shown to an audience, then there might be a small Finnish[*] company that creates wonderful renderings with a simple and easy-to-use tool that anybody can implement on their own CRM. If your needs involve creating a number of dashboards for different audiences, maybe also connecting different database sources, then a small American company[†] might have a low-cost solution that can be easily set up by a consultant in outsourcing in a few hours.

If you need more complex information rendering, of geolocated data, between many branches or business units, then a proper analysis should be put in place as this could be another type of project to deploy, a bit more complex than just a plug-and-play tool.

---

[*] Dear lucy (dearlucy.co).
[†] Slemma (slemma.com).

Chapter 8

Implementing a CRM tool

This chapter is aimed to provide a framework to organisations that are about to plan an implementation project. In analysing the procedure for deploying a customer relationship management implementation project we will go on general terms considering what should be taken into account no matter the digital tool chosen.

Because no two CRM projects are the same, the involvement of an experienced project manager able to empower the Project Steering Committee is strongly recommended. The team of management who should be able to engage all the stakeholders to smooth the way.

The topics covered in this chapter are as follows:

1. Starting a CRM Implementation Project
2. Implementing a CRM Solution
3. Reasons Why CRM Implementation Projects May Fail
4. Summary

Starting a CRM Implementation Project

Everyone knows how implementing a project to develop a custom solution is rarely completely straightforward; even in the most simple cases, the requirements can change along the way and the overall complexity is often underestimated, firstly from the buyer. This is even more true when information technology is involved. Here we believe it would be beneficial to notice how CRM projects are more complex than people generally believe as

DOI: 10.4324/9781003148388-8

they mix technological and organisational challenges. What too often happens is that organisations may consider the CRM implementation project just as a tech matter, giving tech people guidance on how it should work, but they are not prepared to check neither the sales processes nor the strategy execution, something that would help in order to clarify the project purpose. This approach can unfortunately mislead the project: in fact CRM should empower the organisation to execute long-term decisions and not just support a process or collect data. Whether we face a green field adoption or a substitution of an existing solution, it is always the ultimate purpose that should define the requirements of the project.

> *"Systems follow the strategy! A successful CRM system implementation can only occur if the commercial strategy has been well defined in advance. It is not the CRM system that helps in developing the strategy while a correct system can bring it into life making the strategy execution even more transparent and scalable."**

In fact, when it is expected that the CRM system will help in selling more or, even worse, support sales in lack of any structure or formalised process, the project inevitably fails.

Anne Guethoff reports that organisations need external help to define their sales strategy before they proceed to engage in any CRM decision. Because nowadays tech is not the main problem anymore, the issue shifts to business logic and to the expected outcomes instead. Then CRM projects may be more expensive because of that; there are many non-tech costs related to it and organisations are not always prepared for such investment. In any case, technology is there, ready to do anything we would like to achieve. But how to make it happen could be a topic that would be beneficial to clarify in advance. This is the reason why this book only discusses implementation in the last two chapters: before starting to plan implementations we believe every stakeholder should develop a clearer picture of the complexity behind it. When organisations redefine and formalise their business strategy before placing any effort to implement a system, the outcome is significantly better.

Before even thinking about which vendor, and what tool to buy, organisations have to clarify to the Steering Committee how they describe their

---

* Guethoff, A., *Next Level! 8 Elements for the Development of an Integrated Commercial Strategy*, Springer Gabler, 2021.

market presence, what is their sales strategy, how their sales process flows, what the salespeople are expected to do, what metrics they want to measure... Something that too often managers take for granted and do not even enquire about.

Hence we have the first takeaway

> *Before engaging in a CRM implementation project, organisations should take care to define the purposes and decide how the processes will execute the strategy.*

Define a Project Deployment

Projects are often defined by three elements: *Time, Budget* and *Scope*. The usual approach is to define all the three in advance and try to stick with those values—an approach that never really worked. One of them usually slips away, sometimes is the Budget, sometimes is the timing, especially when the Scope changes along the way, but not rarely all the three slide out of control. When it happens the management puts a stop-loss to the budget, it affects the time and the scope inversely.

For definition a waterfall project considers Resources and Scope usually fixed, while Time becomes dependent. The Agile approach reframed this by setting Time and Resources as fixed parameters and letting the Scope depend on them. In Figure 8.1, we can see the Triangle of Project Management.

To clarify it in a CRM implementation project it would be beneficial to set the Budget and the expected timing, sticking with them and adapting the number and nature of features and functions (Scope) to the effective trends.

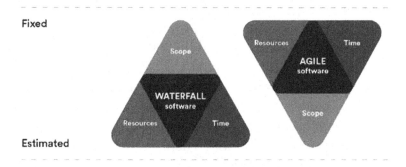

Figure 8.1   The triangle of Project Management.

The reality is that projects are unpredictable per definition, and IT projects can hide complexities that require extra effort from what was planned, and it happens for many (good) reasons. In practice: the Scope of a project concerns how many features and functions can be added to the solution, having made clear that the core purpose of the project is what should be delivered anyway. Hence a project is about *resources, time* and core *deliverables*, while the extent of the Scope (nature and number of deliverables) can vary accordingly with the effort effectively spent on the execution. This approach implies a trade-off between Resources, Time and Scope. What the most relevant of those parameters is, has to be an organisational decision. Some projects need to be closed in time, while others can extend the scope. Is not mainstream but there are also projects where budget is not the limitation.

Let's consider this: CRM projects that cost millions of dollars are not so rare while companies that engaged themselves in those projects were not all of them really keen to invest as much. The Waterfall project management model shows limitations that probably only SAFe is capable of beating.*

Takeaway

> *In planning the CRM project deployment, organisations have to define the main parameters they want to stick with and what will be an acceptable balance of the project's outcomes.*

It doesn't matter if your company is small and the CRM tool you think you need is not that huge; what really matters is the difference between the planned budget and the final cost. Is your company keen to face a 30%, 50% or even 100% increase in the cost of the project? If so, your main parameter can be Time: getting the project done in time is the goal. If the answer is no, then it will be better to put the right effort into analysing and planning carefully before even embarking in the project.

Generally speaking, the features and functions that can be added into a CRM tool can be many and quite complex according to the users' processes, and even a perfect design can be challenged by many requests of additional features that some organisation departments can introduce in the project. On top of that it remains true that availability and quality of features and functionalities can vary between tools. Then, even well-established products

---

* Pereira, D., *Be Careful! SAFe May Be an Undercover Waterfall Agent!*, Medium, 2021

may change, or their inner solutions change more often than you might expect. It means that when a CRM architect designs a solution relying on different available solutions for the feature, at execution it may happen that some adjustments will be required. It can be found faster procedures, with less effort, but more often the effort is greater than planned.

On top of that let's include the possibility that the client can adjust or redefine the requirements, maybe include new ideas, or didn't place enough attention on some kind of data the organisation actually needs, or to the need to shape some information. Or it didn't create issues with data structure that may undermine the output or, last, doesn't make mistakes during the process that require effort to be fixed.

Takeaway

> *Designing everything perfectly before starting is a chimera. It simply doesn't work this way in IT. Being clear about it may help in being prepared for changes that can largely affect the project outcomes.*

But we should also be absolutely aware that an issue can also be the opposite: information technologists are professionals that can rely excessively on the flexibility of the software. At one time it became a quite common procedure to zeroed planning and transfer the clarifications to the execution stage. This happened because it has been perceived that planning is far from perfect, and along the way to execution there are tons of new things that are going to be added. Hence it seems more efficient to just start building and be prepared to adjust everything along the way. But actually this is a false myth that can mislead the project with a critical execution stage in lack of planning. In these cases time becomes a pressing issue as nobody has really assessed the required effort at the planning stage by performing the user's requirements analysis the right way.

Takeaway

> *The right mix of capabilities in planning carefully and deploying safely for a flexible execution is vital in project management that involves software.*

While it can be frustrating when requirements change constantly, the approach to be prepared in tracking those changes, as well as the development of new constraints, is a crucial capability to achieve a clear project outcome that preserves the client's investment and the provider's integrity. Flexibility shouldn't mean chaos and unpredictability. This is the reason why Agile methodology was developed.

There are many outcomes that a CRM implementation project can nurture, even well beyond just the digital tool in place (the output) that enhances productivity. There are other areas that can benefit from the project: it may also offer the opportunity for a strategic alignment. This outcome can have wider implications for the organisation, as it enables a rethinking of how different areas comply with the business strategy.

Any organisation that engages itself in a CRM project can strongly consider it as a breakthrough in its day-to-day operation. A project with a strong impact that creates more problems in the short term may strive to turn it later into a positive impact by enabling more productivity and better control.

Defining What, How and to What Extent

Actually it is the preparation that opens a space for the most relevant opportunities and decisions for the long term, as once the project is launched there will be less time to engage in speculation over what could be. Hence, the time to discuss and make strategic decisions is when the execution is not yet on the agenda.

Deciding what will be the situation once the output is in place can be an exercise of imagination for many organisations; for this reason it can be useful to break the process into small chunks, each of them defined into clear boundaries: what should happen and what would be possible to be done, when and how the process can run automatically and when operators should decide over the process.

Sometimes managers tend to approach the process in its completeness, while operators may have more awareness of its components and the different possible options. It would be useful to describe the process in written form, slicing it into its components, then reviewing them with each stakeholder. Different reviews can alter the single perspective, and even if they confirm it, the process of sharing responsibility on *"what"* the solution will be has a paramount value. The Steering Committee is responsible for the design process, and every department and each stakeholder should contribute to it.

While deciding what has to be done, designers are also involved in verifying how things work. More specifically, what data are collected and how, whether that information has options, structures or formats and how it links into other types of handlings. This verification has an effect on the future use of the fields and how they will interconnect in the system. We can recall that the Data Architecture implies a structure, and fields should be controlled for their possible dataset in order to avoid errors. If a field is designed as a container of numbers, it controls the input that will be just numeric. If later on someone discovers that it would be useful to also include letters, the nature of that field should be changed and its control will be excluded or it will have to be redesigned with a specific format. Hence it is important that the analysis specify the use of the fields to support the data architecture design.

What has to be the data input and the output as information can be simple in its first analysis, but it should also be ready for further uses that are not included in the project scope in the beginning. The easiest way many people use to avoid trouble is to use fields as open strings (Text 255) with no control. In that case any later change won't create problems, but in fact this nullifies the function of data architecture, as it is a total avoidance of rules over inputs. A lack of rules that makes the expected outputs impossible to take under control.

Sometimes organisations fail to realize to what extent their digital infrastructures can affect clients' experience. Broken functionalities, missing periodical testing, slow processing can be perceived as out-of-date, a lack of attention to the customer and a reduced customer centricity that can be more damaging than what the organisation can possibly anticipate. For this reason, planning and executing a proper data architecture can affect not only the efficiency of the data management, but it will also have an impact on the way in which operators use the system, the usability that later will impact how much and how well people will use the system.

One of the greater issues for any CRM digital solutions, especially in the sales departments in business-to-business companies, concerns salespeople who are prone to avoiding using a system as they perceive it as overcomplicated and that requires an extra effort for just admin duties. Salespeople may be more keen to spend extra effort on dealing with client requests than hitting keyboards for the benefit of someone else or to enable the company in tracking their job. Avoiding that perception is paramount. For this reason a great outcome of a CRM implementation project would be to help salespeople in falling in love with the CRM as it effectively empowers them to regain efficiency, get control on their activities and track their own effort and results, first and foremost for their own control. This outcome, as you can see, is not a tech issue, it is mainly a logical approach on how to plan the *What* and *How* of the solution. Technology is not an issue, it is the design of the solution that matters. Knowing the problem to tackle and addressing the right solution is a way to help people feel empowered when using the CRM.

Takeaway

> *Engaging all parties in the organisation in the design process can allow designers to unveil hidden issues by gathering everyone's expectations. Therefore, well beyond just reaching a solution that can fit everyone, the design alignment may support the correct expectations setting.*

What makes this process difficult to accomplish, in general, is time. When faced with time pressure to meet deadlines, designers may find it difficult to interview each stakeholder appropriately and collect data that impact on the system design. Most of the time rushing to complete the process's stage can frustrate the information gathering. Sometimes well-experienced designers are able to enquire in a more effective way by going straight to the point, grasping untold views and issues, and figuring out what would be the most appropriate design. For this reason, the designer's effectiveness really matters for the process result; while some can rapidly develop a picture, others may miss that efficiency, they would require more time and several interviews on the same subject to shape the system for the better. It is in this area that the opportunity to work as a team enables the Project Steering Committee to support each other and improve total effectiveness.

Sometimes the issues of the design process can be influenced by the organisation, when either the management or the employees find it difficult to transfer correct information or knowledge on the sets of data that may help the designers to grasp the picture. This knowledge alignment problem may imply a greater effort of designers to reach a clear understanding, an effort that must be taken into account from the Steering Committee. An effort that, if spent properly, will improve the managers knowledge about the importance of data and how to treat them with care.

Other times there are organisational culture issues that can be hidden behind rules or regulations like the privacy law. In some cases, data privacy barriers can be legitimate, especially in industries like healthcare or banking; in that case a tool that enables data masking technology may be useful during the project deployment, but it is never a good reason to ban designers or IT developers from having access to datasets and procedures.

Takeaway

> *While the value of the analysis is paramount when it is properly run, it can be seriously damaging too if badly handled. And this may be a skill-pattern issue. This would suggest that teams can better organise the analysis when they work efficiently, but also a strong passion for organisational enhancement is strongly required.**

Big Bang or Lean

Organisations can find themselves launching projects upon the CRM when they are already experiencing difficulties: they need a tool in place to organise, smooth and improve complex processes that are already overloaded. And they need it immediately. As everyone knows this is not something odd, or avoidable in any way, it's part of how we work. It is mainly a component of entrepreneurial risk management: picking the chance when it is the right time to invest, avoiding it when the time is not yet. Anyone who is involved in managing at C level knows and understands how difficult it is to hit the fine line between too early and too late. When an organisation decides to launch a project it is often into a complex time already (too late), hence time to analyse, decide and share in the team can be scarce. Then keeping the implementation project as fast as possible is also a way to bear up with the investment.

What can be useful to evaluate then is a different approach from the classic waterfall big bang. What companies often expect is to buy a solution able to fit all their needs. Depending on the organisational complexity the approach can be to deal with the need to find a solution capable to support the whole digital infrastructure of the company. It is often believed that once the implementation stage of a solution is reached, it is better if it includes everything, as that creates an advantage in cost. For this reason people generally think: "Engaging in a sequence of several small projects brings more trouble, it can be more risky, have long delays and there is less confidence in getting the final integrated outcome".

---

* Mintzberg, H., *Why Analysis Is Not Enough and Passion Is So Important, by Karl Moore*, McGill University, Forbes, 2013.

This is an approach that pursues the best from any project, looking at the benefits of a fully comprehensive system deployed in one single project. And it is often among the reasons why organisations very often decide to follow the approach of a *"big bang"* release. They are all good reasons as they try to save money and pursue an omni-comprehensive and quicker result. In a few words, a better investment.

The counter-intuitive approach, better known as Lean, takes risk management into consideration from a different perspective: how sustainable would a project failure be if it involves the whole organisation?

Under this perspective, the Lean approach suggests undertaking smaller projects, reaching their results, evaluating their outcomes, then adjusting and finally launching the next one. From the cost perspective, this way is obviously not cheaper than a single big project. But the benefits are in other domains. First and foremost, risk control is achievable over each small project that only involves just a portion of the organisation and a small amount of resources while its outcome, mostly the learning achievement, is impactful on the sequential strategic decisions.

Everyone who has already applied the Agile methodology is aware of how impactful this method has been for business management at many levels. We can affirm that software and organisational projects are the kind of projects that include many variables and can be easily altered along the way; for this reason applying the Lean and Agile methodologies to them is the best way to go. It helps to avoid embracing investments that could be severe for the organisation in case of failure; instead the recommendation is to proceed by smaller, more suitable steps, measure the outcomes, fix problems that arise, adjust the output and mark the project done. In this case if the project fails it won't hit the organisation badly. If it brings trouble they can be faced and resolved with limited resources. If something isn't what is expected, that is an opportunity to learn while facing a lower level of stress. If the project at the end goes well, everything learned can be applied to the next project. If the project goes wrong, or it fails completely, learning what and why went wrong is essential to avoid more failures. As we all know, projects do have a rate of failure for definition; otherwise they are not projects but processes.

How high is that rate of failure depends on many factors, but in the CRM industry the rate of "unsuccessful" implementations seems to be quite high: some reports consider it well above 65%.* To be fair we should go into detail of that frightening high rate, as Edinger says:

---

* Edinger, S., *Why CRM projects fail and how to make them more successful*, HBR, 2018.

"Those failures can mean a lot of things: Over-Budgeting, Data Integrity Issues, Technology limitations, and so forth. But in my work with clients, when I ask executives if the CRM system is helping their business to grow, the failure rate is closer to 90%"

Nobody would engage themselves in a project that has such a failure rate, but companies nowadays are embracing CRM at the highest rate ever, in accordance with their marketing needs to reach a competitive advantage by differentiating their markets' approach, and the trend seems not to be going to end any time soon.

Takeaway

We believe that the alarm should be given: it is not something to undertake easily, underestimating the complexity and the risk, but it is about learning how to sit among that 10% of successful organisations!

It has to be said that the literature about information technology failures is quite dramatic. In a study from Accenture titled *"Digital Value or Digital Vanity,"* the authors are definitely direct in their warning:

*"It is hard to believe that any company would invest millions in a major transformation without a clear picture of the value delivered. Yet this is happening every day when it comes to digital."**

We can then assume that is not a problem of CRM tools implementation, but this risk seems to affect the whole IT industry. But again, many fail but many don't; we should pursue the strategy to succeed, not run away from risk.

Takeaway

A great way to face high-risk projects is to slice them into small, easily digestible chunks, and manage them for the outcome of learning, while we seek the goal of the correct output. If we do not hit the goal immediately we can then alter it, adjust it or eventually discard it entirely. And the last thing will be more difficult to do if the weight of the investment on the company's balance sheet is too big.

---

* Campagna, C., Arora, S., and Delawalla, A., *Digital Value or Digital Vanity*, Accenture, 2018.

Implementing a CRM Solution

Plans are worthless, but planning is everything.[*]

This statement also aligns with the Agile methodology where outputs can vary, but it is still important to create plans to design the roadmap.

Digital solutions on CRM are also very much that way. Planning doesn't mean having figured out the perfect solution in every detail, but the developing of a quite clear design which is useful for:

1. understanding what is required and what can actually be done; and
2. clarifying how to proceed with stages and milestones settings.

Pre-Setting

A plan starts with an *As Is* evaluation:

■ Where are we and what are we doing right now?
■ How do we do what we do?
■ Why do we do what we do?
■ What are the issues we are stuck with?
■ Where are the major bottlenecks?
■ What do they affect?
■ What is the level of productivity right now?

Organisations that realize they need to change their CRM digital tool can improve their effectiveness by using the process described here. We are not depicting it for consultants or solution providers as they all know how to proceed. Here we focus on managers and entrepreneurs who are keen to learn how to deal with a CRM implementation project even before engaging a consultant or a solution provider company to deploy it. The more the client is aware, educated and conscious about the project and its management topics, the better the client can lead the relationship with all providers and professionals involved in it. The better the client can understand the project issues and problems the better they will be able to avoid them or to solve them in the smoothest way. But mostly, the client can develop, together with all the stakeholders and providers, a better outcome that can fit the organisational expectations.

---

[*] Attributed to: Eisenhower, D.D.

Here we are going to see things from the client's point of view in order to clarify why some stages are important and what they can lead to when they are properly deployed.

"As Is evaluation" means consciousness. If we want to start with a wider approach we could think of how many times we, as persons, believe we know ourselves, who we are, only to discover later that we are not fully aware of it. This happens even more to organisations where the alignment between departments and managers may be missing.

Let's say that the As Is evaluation required to run a CRM project is not about the deeper level of "who we are" but is more about "how we work," how we do what we do and why we believe a CRM tool can help to do it better. Hence starting by sketching down the main points related to our issues and feelings around the area of relationships with clients and how the organisation controls, manages and ultimately leverages them to thrive, is the very first brick of the new building.

The As Is evaluation stage empowers the organisation to establish what can help in improving the situation by setting a difference between a "To Be" description and the initial stage: "Here We Are." But well beyond it, starting by sharing views between stakeholders and highlighting what works and what doesn't, or what can just be improved helps the organisation tremendously in setting expectations and clarifying the real value of each part of the change and which processes are under improvement. The management should leverage this stage by setting five awakening outcomes of it:

1. Setting a better awareness about today's situation. It highlights limits and benefits.
2. Clarifying what should be prioritized with the project. It enables us to define milestones and timing better.
3. Clarifying what works in processes and routines today as it is. Then decide that it should be kept with no changes.
4. What to expect the change would be and in what timing. This may help to figure out either the effort and any second best outcome.
5. What the impact on the organisation will be during and after the change. Set how the organisation may deal with the disruption, reducing people's fear and define better expectations.

Once the pre-setting, the As Is evaluation, is completed, the organisation should be able to define what has to be changed, and how it should be done. In both ways, decisions have to be made as to what works and has to be kept as it is, eventually just transferred into new tools, and what needs to be redesigned thanks to the new tools. Process redesign should be independent of the tool; instead it should lead to a decision about which tool would fit the requirements at the best. Eventually, once it is decided which tool fits better, it can be analysed how what has been planned should be twisted to match with the tool's capability; not everything imagined is convenient to be put in place that way, sometimes, it can be more efficient to alter the design a little to be able to fit the technology.

Takeaway

> *Most of the time managers first buy the tool, then they try to fig-*
> *ure out how to design the processes leveraging the tool templates,*
> *schemes and capabilities. This approach seems logical as it is*
> *mainly by doing that you can understand how you should do it, but*
> *in fact it is limiting as people just stick with the tool approach. They*
> *learn what the tool gives them. Design should be independent of the*
> *tool, and organisations should choose the tool accordingly.*

When companies define their requirements before the tool selection, they generally make a better selection and achieve a most satisfactory project outcome.

It should be clear that nobody would start building a skyscraper by linking pillars and beams to see how to do it. Information Technology has given too many possibilities and that flexibility can lead to seeking short-cuts that allow us to directly build something, supposedly enabling the learning-by-doing.

The Lighthouse

The setting of a project always includes the "To Be" evaluation, only that sometimes it is just taken for granted and the project purposes are set as:

- *"change the CRM to improve our business;"* or
- *"change the CRM to create better relationships with our customers."*

Both are dreams without measurable goals. They are not SMART. Without the possibility to clearly define them it won't be possible to measure how much of them we achieved and if the effort, the investment made, was correct to achieve that.

Let's consider this:

■ The project *output*, the "*To Be*", is where we want to go, the lighthouse of the journey
■ The project *purpose*, the "*What we want*," is the reason why we want to engage in such an effort, the strategy that will lead the journey.

Playing with a little bit of neuro-linguistic programming we would say: "*we want to be at the lighthouse by midnight, as we want to spend the night in it to enjoy the experience of hearing the waves and the wind around the building and the rocks.*"

OK, perhaps it matches very little with a CRM implementation project, but it is the procedure that readers already know to define a goal with the SMART methodology that matters. Why don't we do it all the time? Well, managers are required to deal with many issues and many instances arriving to them from everywhere. This is even more the case for entrepreneurs, as they have their own priorities patterns, in which they rarely list those projects at the top. Hence there can be a focus issue and a time issue; the lack of focus and time can lead people to shortcuts, taking for granted that we are all on the same page.

Let's say that a company always has in place a CRM, even if they may not call it CRM. As we have seen at the very beginning, the CRM is first and foremost a way to be in a relationship with stakeholders. And for it you just need commitment. CRM is the idea and the strategy to be in relationship with clients, either existing or to be.

For that we can consider that an organisation is never deprived of a way to stay in touch with customers. The way in which an organisation achieves that vital duty of the business is what matters, while what enables that relationship is the tool that may probably be not the right one or it can be blunt.

Hence a project around the CRM is one part redefining the strategy, and one part tool definition, design and implementation.

Having this concept clear can definitely help in defining the purpose and the output that a company has to set. If you like you can make an analogy with the mission and vision setting:

■ The *Vision* is what the organisation sees around itself now and then, and that justifies its reason why.

■ The *Mission* is what the organisation wants to achieve in that environment in conformity with the reason why the organisation exists.

Setting vision and mission is less fashionable today than it was years ago. We cannot judge if this is good or bad, but what we do know is that having something clear to share inside and outside the organisation can only help and, in the same way, having something clear to share about and around a project can also help.

Setting a *purpose* that fits with the organisation's strategy, adding value to it is what makes a purpose engaging and valuable for everyone.

The *output* should be the situation where the organisation will find itself when the project will be completed, in terms of tools and methodology of work, which will greatly enhance its effectiveness and then the business.

Planning the Project Deployment

Once the project is set, it will be time to decide what technology to involve, if it is to be a scratch development or a platform, a LowCode platform or a CRM platform, that enables the development or even a pre-built framework.

Technology matters in terms of planning; when and how each component should be developed can definitely change when using different technologies.

Let's leave aside what matters for each single project development planning; let's analyse what is always true, in the confidence that every project manager will lead the technology adoption for the best. We will talk about solutions in the last chapter.

Data Architecture

Working on the dataset can be the very first task to set in order to clarify the next stages. Facing how and where the data are displaced into the existing methodology and tool matters to redesign a dataset that will fit into the new technology. Each solution has a way to displace and use data. It is partially a technology legacy and partially is due to the methodology applied to it. Anyone who has experienced dealing with the migration from spreadsheets into a digital CRM platform knows how the use of a spreadsheet can be tricky in terms of fields and dataset.

To clarify: datasheets are composed by the first line of columns' titles (field names) and each row is a record which stores the data of each contact/element.

When people create a database on a spreadsheet, what they do is name each column with a title and store in the cell the unidimensional value.

```
CLIENT = YES/NO
DATE OF CLIENT = 01/02/2020
PURCHASE = ITEM A
DATE TO PURCHASE = 03/02/2020
PURCHASE 2 = ITEM B
DATE TO PURCHASE 2 = 08/08/2020
PURCHASE 3 = ITEM C
DATE TO PURCHASE 3 = 03/02/2021
ADDRESS = 20 Manchester Street, DE22 3GB Derby, United Kingdom
COUNTRY = UK
REGION = ~~EUROPE~~? ROW
```

(this is just a simple example to highlight the type of issue)

As you can see there is a redundancy of data even in this simple, short dataset. Let's try to explain: here the origin of the data was to enable the selection of records (contacts) that show existing clients, excluding anyone who is not a client. Then the idea was to know when a contact became a client to be able to separate them by the length of the relationship. Then having the information of the purchasing history. Then the full address. And just to make things "simpler" a field for the country and one for the geographical region.

Now let's consider some issues:

1. Is the field "client" really necessary? No, as there are purchases done with the dates.
2. Is the date becoming client necessary? No, as purchasing history has the dates (first purchase matches the change of status: client yes)
3. Is the field "country" necessary? Nope, as that information already exists in the address
4. Is the field "region" necessary? No. OK, the UK has just changed its status from a European country to a Rest Of the World one, but this information can be set dynamically in a different way: let's imagine that the purpose of the creation of this field was to select marketing areas as EMEA, the fit of UK into "EMEA" or even into a "Europe" group can be done by a query that selects the list of countries that match the group. To clarify: a query capable of selecting all the records that have as country in the address any country that matches with the group selection ("Europe" or "EMEA" in this case). Is it definitely more complex but when something changes you have to change only the query one time,

not every record that has the unidimensional data in (Europe). But even more important is the reduced input effort that also impacts on errors reduction.

5. Is the list of purchases necessary? Nope. Instead of setting a list of (eventually manually managed) items in a spreadsheet, it would be much more efficient to create a system of related tables: something quite common indeed.

Now, if you think that medium-size enterprises do not use spreadsheets well, forget it. Medium-size and small enterprises often use similar approaches, because at the end of the day medium-size businesses were small companies not long ago.

This was only an example, a very basic one, made using the spreadsheet as the basis of data, but the problem is not limited to spreadsheet use. Notwithstanding how much people keep using spreadsheets, namely MS Excel, as databases, it can be quite impressive to learn that the problem of bad data management is everywhere. Database logic and know-how is something not widely shared, while shortcuts such as using a simple spreadsheet to collect data is what people have often accepted as a standard. But even when a database is in place it is not guaranteed that its design is effective and efficient, or it strongly depends on its first stage development. To understand why the data architecture must be reviewed not only primarily, but every time the technology changes, we should evaluate its impact on the effectiveness of fields' usage. On top of that let's think about the legacy of the previous data architecture design: who did that? Why? For what specific use was it built at that time? What changes have been applied since? Who did them?

The result is often a cluttered dataset that requires to be redesigned not only because of the new technology, but also because over time it became so cluttered by adding unnecessary fields and so full of bad data that its usability can be crippled.

Then we should consider the available dataset: the importance of what can be stored in the fields for boosting efficiency in the system management. An efficiency that can be achieved by leveraging on the design of the data architecture (see Chapter 3).

Let me be clear: even dirty data can be used in a business intelligence tool and, by that, develop a rendering of useful information, but mounting an analysis of a cluttered and dirty database is much more difficult, complex and time consuming than reaching an even better output by working on a cleaner dataset in a well-designed database.

Unfortunately, working to clean databases of bad data is not perceived as valuable, and its marginal value is probably not really sensible for some businesses, but the importance of redesigning the data architecture for a new approach when the technology changes should be clear to everybody.

Takeaway

> *Less is more. This is true also with the number of fields of a database. Information is not better shaped by a plethora of fields, and the best way to build information rendering over data includes: reliable and unique data collected within parameters clearly defined and easily adjustable. There is an optimal quantity of fields for each database purpose, everything more than that creates a problem.*

Dirty Data

One example of bad data for databases (CRM) can be reported from booking platforms. You can imagine how many transactions are recorded on a standard platform, how many records about hosts and guests are continuously updated from many different sources: payments systems, registration forms, hotel databases, social media, travel agencies and the list can go on as long as you like.

Let's imagine all these databases. How many times do they have the same person or the same hotel (host) listed in, and how many different denominations can they have? For one single person, for instance, how many email addresses can be registered, some also wrongly copied, how can we check that person is not the same one that booked last year in that very same hotel? Or maybe the one that left unpaid damage in another hotel two weeks ago?

And the list of hotels is not much different: hotels can be denominated in many ways—*The Franklin Hotel, Franklin hotel, The Franklin London Hotel, Starhotels Franklin,* etc., and also their addresses: */24 Egerton Gardens, Chelsea, London SW3 2DB / Egerton G. London / Egerton gardens 24, Chelsea / etc.*

OK, now you have just put a foot in the water: data management is very complex even at this very shallow level.

The complexity of data is also related to the data life: for how long are some data still valid? What changes take place and how can it be possible to match previous data with new, changed ones?

For this purpose there exist some specific software that can match entire, even huge databases, and enable data matching, data analysis and updates that would be simply impossible to manage by hand.

But plan data architecture is something that can't be delegated to any software: designing how the new dataset should be organised is mainly a human know-how (still), while organising the previous data for the new architecture is a task that some software can support.

Takeaway

> *GIGO: Garbage In, Garbage Out, is a golden rule. If an organisation is about to invest in a new CRM, it should also imply a data review. The data architecture and the database cleaning are investments that can pay back later while using the new technology.*

Data are the kernel of the CRM, both as a tool and as a strategy. But the quality of data represents the backbone of the information that can be shaped around the environment, the markets and the organisation's performance.

It is often wrongly believed that a base of data is something just stored somewhere and useful to pick up when required. This conviction can dramatically limit the capability of the organisation to leverage its own asset: the ownership of a base of data achieved along the way with years of interaction with clients and creating value to them. If data is the major valuable asset nowadays, taking care of them should be an obvious consequence of the process of enhancing our own capability to nurture the business through the relationship with the markets.

Process Workflows

Workflows are the sequence of steps involved in moving from the beginning to the end of a working process.* A workflow is the execution, manual or automated, of (business) processes, in which tasks, information and documents move from A to B as the consequence of actions under a set of

---

* Definition from Merriam-Webster.

procedural rules. It can involve work done or decisions made by people or it can be fully automated, and its purpose is to transform materials, information or services.

> *A workflow consists of an orchestrated and repeatable pattern of activity, enabled by the systematic organization of resources into processes that transform materials, provide services, or process information. It can be depicted as a sequence of operations, the work of a person or group, the work of an organization of staff, or one or more simple or complex mechanisms.**

Essentially the CRM tool's design involves the detailed design of business processes, in which the digital tool plays an important role: enabling, controlling and verifying each workflow and the whole process. The tool should also be capable of facilitating speed enhancement and error reduction, and ultimately producing reliable results in a more productive environment.

Each process design covers each workflow design; a process can contain many sub-workflows, each with a start and an end. Starts are triggered by an event or an input while the end defines a new state, as an information update or a service provided. An end of one workflow provides an output, and that output can produce a human decision or action, generally outside the organisation, that induces a new trigger. The new event triggers the start of another workflow. This circle of workflows, triggered by events and producing outputs that cause new triggering events, leads to the creation of the final output of the whole process.

This is the case of the sales process (see Chapter 3), where different stages are enabled by some events and they lead into a new status. The design of the sales process includes a preview of triggers and outputs: what *can* happen and what *should* be the effect.

In terms of micro-details, at the design stage the main purpose is to know how the workflow should work, if that can be done by a click or by drag and drop or even by an automated procedure. This is something that can be decided at the digital tool implementation time. At the design stage, it could be useful to know what would be useful to automate so that the selection will shortlist tools that can provide that capability.

The most important workflows are in vital processes like Sales and Customer Support but also Marketing and Administration. According to the

---

* Definition from Wikipedia.

type of business, the production can include processes controlled or that include some CRM functions. CRM implementation is about creating all those workflows that compose each process.

Takeaway

> *Organisations can pursue more successful projects by planning CRM implementations sliced into sub-projects for each process, focusing on making all its workflows work. Then move to the next process.*

Making automation work is great and the more automations are in place the more each workflow can save time for people, and enhance productivity. At the beginning of the implementation it could be beneficial to apply an Agile approach: first deploy the process with a minimal—safe—degree of automation, then run it manually to observe and learn what works and what could create issues. Once this knowledge is acquired, one automation can be introduced and tested on a larger, fuller scale. Then the next setting begins, a new automation is introduced, tested and deployed, and so on. Working incrementally strongly boosts the organisational know-how.

Takeaway

> *Incremental building is like constructing a means of travel, starting with assembling a bicycle, then a moped, after that a motorbike and later a car. Trying to build a car in the first place can be an excess of effort and, in lack of an effective know-how, probably also too risky.*

Processes and workflows are the basics of any digital CRM and their perfect execution allows organisations to pursue a productivity enhancement. To avoid failures while implementing automation in workflows, companies can proceed by stages allowing the right time to reach the final status, because embracing shortcuts can create issues that later won't be easy to detect where they originated from.

CRM Outputs

Every process involves inputs which are intended for creating outputs. The CRM is a complex of processes, each of them with different outputs, which all converge into one main output: the business.

Each business is a process where resources are collected, utilised and transformed into products or services that create and deliver value to customers. CRM as a tool can govern a portion of the whole process or even a big part of the processes that together compose the business process. Hence defining what the outputs of each process are, is a design matter that finds its final verification at the implementation stage. Outputs are generally information, bearing the shape of documents, either digital or solid, or services that can include goods.

On this basis, the team working on the implementation stage should take care that the outputs planned at the design stage are effectively delivered in time and consistency as expected.

Outputs are not set in stone; flexibility on how they should be composed, what they should contain and how they should be delivered is important as the requirements can vary depending on the business stage. It can also happen that outputs' requirements vary along the implementation deployment, and this can't be dismissed by the implementation team. But on the other hand changes shouldn't be easily adopted, because of a lack of clear requirements' change they can lead to confusion. The result in that case could be a chaos where nobody is able to decide if the failure is connected to the system, the design or something else.

Decision-Making

Among outputs are also included all the information rendering that the analytics over the CRM tool can provide. In Chapter 7, we read about the reporting and forecasting that the implementation team should develop over the course of the CRM implementation project. Due to the specific essence of information rendering, it is a good practice to collect a quantity of data that can support enough charts and reports before even starting implementing the analytics tool.

The selection of the right analytic tool and its implementation can be a quite specialised task as such a tool can differ a lot from the CRM tool. This stage is a project in itself and can be standing alone independently.

The importance of providing reliable and accurate information to decision-makers relies on the quality of the tool and its internal algorithms management: a tool where users are supposed to trust what happens inside without being capable of control is not acceptable ever. But it is also very much dependent on the implementation of the stage in terms of plan and settings. Engaging a BI team when the project is big enough can generate better results than trying it in-house.

A rule is always remarkable: *Less is More.*

- Develop renderings and charts incrementally to help control the results and the processes behind them.
- Decide what metrics to track to build the information pattern that will provide concise, concrete dimensions to operate on.
- Develop dashboards with a few coherent charts about a cluster of metrics related to each other instead of putting everything together.
- Create dashboards for different users and recipients using different methodologies, which will be concise and plain to financial staff, clean and straight to sales teams, engaging for investors and the external stakeholders.

Takeaway

Working on information rendering is not just about presenting data; the data collated into charts should be able to tell a story, to explain from where to where the business is moving. Data scientists generally focus on rendering stories accessible and understandable by non-technical people. It is important to think about recipients and what they expect to find from such an abundance of data. The capability to reduce them to a bite-size quantity without changing their nature or meaning relies on a fine line of know-how, intentions, business knowledge and ethical behaviour. This is why a heterogeneous team can achieve it better.

Reasons Why CRM Implementation Projects Fail

Project Management standards consider that any project can fail, and the rate of missing success can vary according to the domain of the project. It also depends on the evaluation parameters: if we strictly consider all the parameters as constraints then probably 99% of projects don't produce the expected results. If we consider the whole outcome of a project, including the learning achievement, then probably that rate drops to 1%.

Is it then only a matter of requirements settings or flexibility in evaluation?

Of course not. Very few people will be happy, and no CFO will, if an expensive project fails to deliver anything useful, even if the learning account records massive inbound. Nurturing the learning accounting is great; it is something that every organisation should do. Unfortunately, it just can't be done any longer, only burning resources. Some complete failures are part of organisational life, but they are still painful and not in the scope of any organisation. We can be happy to learn that something can't work that way and test some other way to make it work, but that is different from accepting a complete failure.

> *"However, the price tag for the project has exceeded the $1 billion planned and significant damage was done to the company's reputation and its financial performance."**

Setting requirements, constraints and expectations is still important; knowing how to play with them by bending them according to changing situations and chances can be extremely important to set the basis for success or failure. On one hand, this defines the evaluation framework ex-post: the stricter it is, the less variance in defining what can be successful is allowed. On the other hand, this approach can affect project management and people's decision-making by introducing fears and rigidness that quite often mislead the choices. It can also induce a risk-averse mode that can frustrate the project's amplitude and output.

The case of big failure quoted before from Bligh and Turk's *CRM Unplugged*[†] includes *"However..."*. In the end the company achieved the goal of speeding up processes and reducing errors that were in place before the implementation; they managed to achieve better customer satisfaction by speeding up processes, but it did cost them much more than expected, both in direct cost and in revenue loss, without mentioning the loss of reputation.

Takeaway

> *This tells us that having a big budget in place cannot ensure a company's ability to avoid dreadful failures. It only tells us that most of the time big corporations can cope with huge losses better than medium-sized enterprises, but no one is shielded against big debacles.*

---

* Bligh, P., and Turk, D., *CRM Unplugged*, Wiley, 2004.
[†] Ibidem.

Moreover, there are specific elements that impact CRM implementation projects and that it would be useful to be aware of, learn how to control or, even better, entirely avoid. They are related to four main areas:

- Mission Setting
- Design and Planning
- Leadership Commitment
- Implementation Undertaking

Mission Setting

Under this class fall several items that matter for the definition of the project's

- Purpose
- Scope Width
- Expectations Setting

To avoid issues with the project mission's setting, the project Steering Committee should take account of needs and requirements of the organisation, run an As-Is analysis, depict the solution and then come back to the "client" with a clear view of what can be done and how the output will be. Explain how the output will fit the needs and requirements (Purpose) and to what extent the solution will cover the needs (Scope). This procedure engages people in getting responsibility of it (Expectations).

In the absence of a project scoping document shared with stakeholders, each new requirement would be considered as part of the project and added without an evaluation of its impact on the project itself.

Purpose

The project's *Purpose* concerns the clarification of what is expected *"To Be."* What should be the situation after the implementation. This picture can often be defined vaguely or in lack of measurable metrics. Having a SMART goal in mind can help to share clearer milestones and deliverables and develop awareness on how much still left to be done. If the output is not clearly defined anything that comes across can disturb the perception of the match between the expected result and effective output.

*Even more importantly, it has been hypothesised that the greatest num-
ber of failures happen due to lack of alignment between project purpose and
strategy.*

Scope

The project's *Scope* also falls in the previous category: lack of alignment.
What will be included in the project output and why, what can be added
or removed to stick with the budget or timing are part of the initial settings
about the output.

*Scope also governs the control of a tendency to just try to automate exist-
ing processes without addressing redundancies, outmoded practices and
problems that stick into the business processes sometimes due to lack of
awareness of them.**

Expectations

The organisational *Expectations* settings has a double function that needs to
be properly clarified. First, we can set them around the imagined output and
the benefits of it; second, we can shape expectations to fit with the output
under design, avoiding paving the way for excessive, unreal expectations
beyond the actual benefits. Controlling Expectations is an essential part of
the design process, and its roots are entangled in the As-Is analysis.

*A lack of a proper process of shaping expectations where designers enter
into details of processes, can affect whether possible changes and improvements will be considered part of the project (and its budget) by the client.*

Design and Planning

Designing the solution in detail is probably the simplest part of the project.
If the client requirements' collection has been run rigorously then the design
should flow. It requires deciding what technology to involve, which of the
existing platforms to use or if the solution should include development from
scratch (and if so in which coding technology). In both cases, it will be
relevant to rely on technology experts who can provide clear answers on
how the technology can fit the first draft. After having achieved some clarity about the possible technologies' pros and cons, the selection should be

---

* Bligh, P., and Turk, D., ibidem.

discussed by the Steering Committee who will approve the most balanced choice. Only then a proper design will take place and the planning of what elements, features and functionalities should be developed by their dependencies and interdependencies hierarchical priorities.

At that point the plan of what and when takes a direct value on cost control. The client would need to activate some functions in order to take advantage of an earlier delivery time and start using them. Only if the planning is done correctly will it be possible to answer in terms of possible options. Some functionalities can be developed before others, some can't. Some features require a hierarchy.

To take control over possible issues designers should be able to stick to an exasperating attention to detail and a tedious precision on process analysis and description to be able to depict each designed stage. Something that always pays off in IT, where if it is true that the execution can vary and find better solutions to what has been conceptualised, it also should start with some solid roots on what is expected. Then enabling the executors in finding a different fit to the requirements can be valuable.

A risk would be to fall in the false Agile approach that only relies on the executor to find a solution to any requirement. The idea is that because the executor can use flexibility in developing the solution, it would be convenient not to bother too much in the planning phase with what should be done but, instead, let the executors interpret what the client needs. This approach, indeed very common in small projects, actually introduces uncertainty and unattended effort for back and forth communication that can frustrate decision-making and ultimately produce a different output from what could be expected.

Leadership Commitment

This area includes leadership on the project as well as organisational leadership. If the first one matters for the management of the project, it is the second one that gives power to the project management and down to the organisation to endorse and support the project. In fact the company's leadership can easily ditch the entire venture just showing lack of interest in the project purpose.

Purposes and strategy misalignment is probably one of the most relevant causes for failure in CRM implementation projects. It has been reported that the overwhelming majority of organisations fail in keeping their goals aligned to strategy. In missing alignment compromises arise and decision-making becomes difficult, projects delay and they just crawl to the end unable to meet the stakeholders' expectations.

The whole management should be involved in the CRM project, even if it is deployed in smaller chunks and is not yet extended to the whole organisation. The role of the Steering Committee relies on its composition: stakeholders from every department and key executive should contribute to the decision-making with no exceptions. A Steering Committee crippled can provide choices that are not balanced and they can be felt as a sub-optimal compromise. Contributing to the Steering Committee is a long marathon, not a sprint. To avoid the committee getting stuck or losing influence it is important that members remain in charge at all times and, mostly, they keep engaged and motivated to bring the project to life. This is an effect of creating smaller projects, per stage, that are easy to deploy. After each stage delivery the team can have a break and members can focus on other priorities to be able to come back later recharged and with new ideas. If the substitution of committee members or line managers should happen along the way, the top leadership should ensure that the new executives engage themselves into the project even better than the previous ones.

It can be too easy for new managers to dismiss former decisions with good reasons; they may have a better background or even just the need to prove themselves to be better. If that happens, the risk of failure increases dramatically as a direct effect.

Compensation and Rewards

Rewards and compensations are also extremely important for the project's success, and they rely on tracking performance. Measuring the project trends using its main metrics is the procedure that often lacks firm implementation. Even if everybody knows that it is possible to improve only what we can measure, that great formulation is often bypassed. If a measurement of outcomes is in place and the Steering Committee's members and anyone else involved in the project are properly compensated, the project deployment can move towards the end with more confidence. Rewarding people is a matter well beyond just the financials and it belongs to each organisational culture archetype; how it impacts on project failure/success rate is probably not appreciated enough. Using tools like *"The Celebration Grid"** can enable

---

* Appelo, J., *Managing for Happiness*, Wiley, 2016.

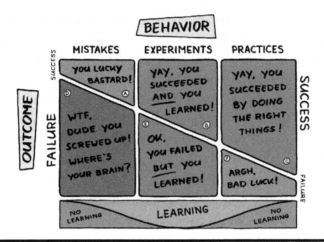

Figure 8.2 Jurgen Appelo, "The Celebration Grid," Managing for Happiness.

management to publicly distinguish behaviours that produce positive outcomes and have to be recognised and rewarded (Figure 8.2).

Reward for successes and contributions can be a tricky aspect of management and leadership. To ditch any project is enough to reward people just on success no matter how. Opportunistic behaviours are extremely common and supporting them by wrong compensation is even more common in organisations.

Business Units CRM

In Chapter 3 we already mentioned that each type of business has its sales process. The sales process is what matters in order to design the CRM pipeline. If a company includes several branches or business units that have different ways to serve markets, then their requirements will differ. The holding should ensure that every system in use, wherever and whatever it is, can report adequately and be able to transfer data and information to its central business intelligence. Or ensure that the tool chosen is flexible enough to work with different pipelines and manage different sets of data and approaches.

Deciding centrally one platform, one tool designed as corporate to fit everyone can frustrate the needs of some business units, reducing its acceptance and usage by people in sales.

Salespeople Engagement

Keeping the focus on the purpose that effectively creates value for customers is an organisational commitment. To be able to truly get the benefits of the effort spent in the CRM project, organisations should stick with a clear mission to bring competitive advantages to the business; investing in wrong areas can reduce the focus on what is truly important for the business growth.

When the CRM implementation includes procedures and routines that do not add any improvement to the customer experience or do not enhance the value delivered, probably it wouldn't move the salespeople. If a fancy layout misleads the team from a correct evaluation of its value in terms of changes of pre-existing, often out-of-date, procedures, the project will fail. Organisations can find themselves spending effort on just re-automating practices that do not provide any competitive advantage for the business. This can lead to over-customizing the features of the CRM, bringing on technical challenges, reducing the usability without getting the expected outcomes.

Salespeople need tools to simplify their job, make them work smarter, enable them to be more efficient in managing their deals along the sales process, and not provide this as part of the CRM will determine a reduced usage and, when possible, avoidance.

Execution Failures

Also well-planned CRM implementations can face unexpected complexities comprising many issues and unforeseen problems. Some problems arise in managing resources related to the project impacting on risk reverberation, finance... Use of the standard of methods like Project Management and Agile, adequate analysis and planning, interferences on the scope planning can help to mitigate problems.

If the Steering Committee is not adequately balanced between departments, namely when there is too much influence in place from one side to the detriment of others, or when the tech department becomes central to the project.

Technology is generally not a problem per se, but when the project is driven mainly by IT specialists an excessive tech-confidence and a lack of "reason why" and purpose focus becomes the risk. Unbalanced power in the management team can steer the project in favour of the more influential one.

Key Points

- Compose a remarkable strategic mission that impacts the bottom line and engage the whole organisation with it.

- Avoid time shortcuts that lead to inadequate design, planning and missing of scope setting; keep the design, the planning and the scope always clear.
- Reduce the scale of each project, slicing a big one into sub-projects, and apply the Agile Project Management method to ensure a controlled flexibility.
- Avoid siloing the decision-making process by engaging everyone in taking part in the outcomes and the change management.
- Empower the leaders to improve the organisational culture and the management methodology to facilitate the pursuit of better results.
- Stick with designed and planned features and functionalities to avoid extending or changing the solution during the execution.
- Allow time to warm-up the organisation in using the tool; offer proper training to people and support the transition for an adequate time frame.
- Avoid over-invest in non-strategic processes; this is the key to keep focusing on value creation.
- Be careful not to miss the opportunity to review processes if that will arise as a need even if it is considered slightly out of scope.

Conclusion

Surveys on CRM tool success continue to show a high rate of misfit in organisations. On the other hand, surveys on the benefit of digital transformation show that 85% of US companies report digital tools helped their businesses in some way.* What is remarkable now is that actually Digital Transformation is becoming a Digital Journey where organisations are involved with their entire being. Some minor fall is part of every journey, but the competitive advantage that a company creates by running a conscious learning process on deploying an implementation project of the CRM is paramount.

---

* Deloitte, *The Performance of Small and Medium Sized Businesses in a Digital World*, 2019. https://www2.deloitte.com/content/dam/Deloitte/es/Documents/Consultoria/The-performance-of-SMBs-in-digital-world.pdf.

Summary

In this chapter, we went through the implementation of the CRM as a digital tool, converging all the approaches and methodologies listed in the previous chapters. The idea of starting with a proper design, then planning the deployment and finally starting the implementation is like a journey: when well prepared and considered in all its risks and opportunities it can be amazing, fulfilling and inspiring; if not, it can turn into a nightmare.

Organisations should be aware they can make it great when:

■ They do not underestimate the effort;
■ They have a clear, viable, sustainable and valuable purpose;
■ They consider carefully the ROI;
■ They are not keen to embrace shortcuts to save time and effort;
■ They support the project under a solid organisational culture;
■ They are ready to engage a Steering Committee, delegating to it enough power;
■ Possibly they are not in rush to finish the project;
■ Eventually they can afford a failure and to ditch the project (or parts of it);
■ Leadership is committed and confident in elevating the organisation to another level.

In wondering if implementation issues can be controlled, a contribution arrives from Michael Muse, a Texan operations software consultant, who wrote about struggle in CRM adoption:

"Why is This Happening?"

You should approach software adoption problems like a Product Manager. If the team isn't using something, the user doesn't understand or appreciate its value.

How do you fix that?

■ Market the utility to the end user.
■ Make it easier to use and quicker to reap said utility.

Easier said than done, right? "You don't know these people!" Wrong. Try this:

■ **Do Some Beta Testing**

Isolate a team that will give thoughtful and direct feedback. Have them do two or three practice runs, and write down what they say. Did they groan while putting in a particular piece of information? Press on, find out why.

■ **Diagnose and Solve**

Did they just find it pointless to put in the data? Write a short, articulate sales pitch of how it's going to help them later. Note: if you can't do this easily, they're probably right and you need to kill the feature. Even if a process mostly serves their manager, figure out how to connect their manager's success to their own, their team's, whatever. People like to understand why they have to do things.

■ **Avoid Common Pitfalls**

It's easy for even a veteran to make common adoption mistakes. When I've hired for Sales Ops in the past, I inevitably ask about a time where adoption was poor, and what the candidate did. The worst answers involve making validation rules, required fields or other quality of life sacrifices. Even worse: "if they don't do it, they don't get paid," The best answers are user-centric."*

---

* Muse, M., *100% CRM adoption never struggle again*, Medium, 2018.

Chapter 9

How to Select a CRM Platform

Technology is not the problem once it is correctly defined. The issue with customer relationship management digital tools, and probably with many digital solutions that companies can decide to adopt for their business, is rarely just a tech issue. Most of the time an unsuccessful outcome, and even more a successful one, can be related to the pattern of choices, behaviours and organisationational culture in place. Either as drivers of the decisions or as parameters to adapt the selected tool upon them, the role of the leadership can be paramount.

The topics covered in this chapter are as follows:

1. Introduction to the Selection Process
2. Selecting the Technology
3. CRM Platform types
4. Vendors List
5. Summary

Introduction to the Selection Process

Most of the time organisations need to learn by experience, starting from using something, then improving and adapting to evolved needs and purposes. In this final chapter, we will develop a thoughtful guide to help management to define the technology and get oriented among the jungle of possibilities. We do not suggest any specific solution; rather our purpose would be to guide everyone who is interested in getting more aware and

DOI: 10.4324/9781003148388-9

performing more conscious decision-making. Let's clarify that the best solution doesn't exist, this is per definition. We just offer to the readers what we learnt along the way and our limited point of view on the possibilities around.

Anyone who has reached this point already has an idea of what is relevant for running a successful CRM implementation project based on what has been outlined in the previous chapters. Now is the time to provide just an overview of some solutions that can serve as a comparison to everyone's self-orientation in order to develop better decision-making. We are also confident that every project manager experienced in CRM implementation projects can develop a more tailored selection of possible solutions based on the specific client's requirements. Here we rank a short list of solutions, to figure out some main differences. The list is totally arbitrary and incomplete as it is intended only to give an idea of how to proceed in a selection process.

Selecting the Technology

Believe it or not, the first choice is about technology. Having cleared the pros and cons of CRM platforms and low-code platforms is the first step. We are not considering here the third option, a development from scratch, which even if technically possible may be in fact absolutely not useful to consider. Using a low-code platform is like starting from scratch, all possibilities remain achievable, but requires some knowledge and quite a lot of work in developing every detail, while a CRM platform can be less flexible but provide an initial framework to support further development.

Low-code technology can be good for creating something that is not available in the market, like some processes that are very company-specific. Even if the use of flexible, open platforms of low coding is growing lately, we will refer mainly to CRM platforms that represent the most common technology for the industry nowadays. When people refer to "CRM" what they really think is a digital, off-shelf solution that functions as a CRM. Among CRM platforms we can divide the used approaches between a more flexible one, where more customisations are easily available, and a more rigid one, where customisations are limited or achievable only by deep coding. Almost all the entry-level tools have limited customisation as they are conceived as off-the-shelf products in pre-built frameworks.

Pre-built frameworks are essentially products ready to use that reduce the implementation effort. Users are facilitated working into a framework of processes and features, interacting with pre-defined, almost rigid user's interface. These products rely on a structure, a layout and their preferences to focus upon one (or several) process(es). Their limitations are always annoying clients, but in some way they are part of the "convenience" of the solution, and those limitations can be considered as elements of the design that are possible to overcome. It is interesting to see that those can sometimes be limitations only under a certain point of view. These ready-to-use tools offer affordable pricing, especially for their entry tier. A different story can be when performance, features and functionalities are required to perform a complete process management. For some vendors also API use is not for free, creating a hidden cost on future development. In the market it is easy to find solutions proposed as completely ready to use, they claim a sort of "plug and play" for their solutions. This is, in our point of view, quite an issue: the message that an organisation can install a software and go, is a strong, probably imprecise but catchy, marketing message. Some types of entry-level CRM tools plug-and-play are gaining popularity as they allow significant saving either in the set-up and in running costs. There are also solutions among them that, often positioned as easy to use, could be appropriate also for companies with more complex requirements.

Also, being entry level doesn't necessarily mean bad, often limited; if an organisation doesn't necessarily need to use such a complexity in its processes, probably a simple, basic and easy to use CRM can work even better than complex, extensive platforms. It is only a matter of selecting the vendor with care, as said there are in the market many, maybe too many, vendors. What makes the difference, easy to say, is their "reason why". If they know what they do (the founders' story matters) then probably their solution can be good. If they add CRM to their solutions just because it is fashionable, then better to stay away. Some small and also medium-sized vendors could run the risk of having developed their solution upon a limited know-how of the real use, then they should prove that their product matches real-life organisational needs.

Decision-Making about CRM Platforms

Entry-level CRMs are also very useful when an organisation focuses the use of the CRM on one or few processes. It is the case in sales in which a lot of vendors offer tools for sales process management, and sometime just for that. Those solutions can also be decent on that specific process. As long as they can be integrated into a system infrastructure that enables data transfer to other organisational functions' tools, they can be useful with their focus on one single process. Often a focused tool may give even better results when developed upon one specific process: a vendor that places all its efforts focusing on improving one process, it is committed to create value to a portion of the whole business process, can be able to reach a remarkable outcome. These laser-focus solutions can be extremely well developed around the end users' experience and they may recognise it as useful for their needs.

This may be an ecosystem approach where a central focused solution runs very well just one part of the whole business process while work integrated with other vertical solutions shaping, this way, the whole company's digital infrastructure. This has been even easier nowadays with the tremendous growth of cloud computing, which has simplified the development of connectors.* Cloud computing is creating huge opportunities for customers and vendors, in terms of possible process control that were almost impossible before. In particular using Application Programming Interface (API) between virtually any software.

When we talk about CRM tools, we only discuss cloud-based solutions, on-premise solutions still existing, but they are out of the scope of this book, and honestly we do not believe there is any good reason to pursue that technology nowadays.

> *"I've never been a fan of the all-in-one CRM tools that have tons of features you'll pay for but never use and fulfill 80% of your needs and still don't move the needle for your business. Most people say they need a CRM because all of their competitors have one, because their sales team is overwhelmed, or because they heard a sales pitch about a tool that was going to 10x their business (who doesn't want their business to be multiplied by 10?) So, why do you need a CRM? You want to increase sales, make customers happier, and make things easier for your team, right? I want to show you how you can build your own super-powered CRM that will serve your needs and no one else's, will cost next to nothing, and work the way you work.*†

Not all the needs can be met by off-shelf solutions. As mentioned, it is true that almost anyone can build a CRM digital solution; starting from scratch, hard coding, or using low-coding platforms, anyone has to decide the strategic value of the tool and primarily the value of their own time and resources. Just the point often undervalued: "cost nothing" is only possible when your own business values nothing. In any other cases if someone uses

---

* Goss, K., *Automate It with Zapier*, Packt, 2021
† Meisel, A., *You don't need a CRM*, Medium, 2018.

time to make it, that time is either paid or stolen by probably more efficient and more valuable allocations. This decision is completely up to each entrepreneur and their own idea of time value.

Personally I'm not passionate about free-stuff anyway, if nothing else because I have never been able to find the answer to a simple question: "*Why would someone give anything valuable away for free?*" Of course anyone would enjoy a free meal, but if you want to be in charge of your own choices (and your own diet), then you probably would prefer to pay than just take what is given to you for free.

> "*I can't tell you how many times a customer would call me saying a vendor announced they are going to End of Life the current version of their cloud offering and now the customers are forced to migrate and absorb the expense or kick off an RFP process to evaluate new vendors. Most, if not all, of these cases resulted from the customer not doing the proper due diligence on the platform during their initial evaluation process.*"*

Luckily the larger market demand is not from companies that seek to build their tools for free. Of course anyone who loves the idea of paying nothing may pursue it and probably, sometimes, in some particular business stages it might also be the right choice. If later on, the business' growth will show that choice limits they will be always able to migrate to a more professional tool. Something that also makes sense if conscientiously using a Lean Approach. In that case most of the tips we provided earlier in this book take an even more remarkable value: being aware of developing your own, maybe temporary, solution, being able to set the data architecture carefully in the most correct way, enables you to reduce migration's headaches later. The learning achievements that are possible by that experience are also very relevant, the next solution that will be chosen will probably be developed inspired by a greater know-how. The greatest decision-making about it is to decide, not really if you have got the right skill for it, but first and foremost how much your own time values (even more as allocation opportunity). Everyone as a business person should be aware of the golden rule to delegate tasks that are below the value of their time. Delegate or outsource them to specialists that can be more efficient and/or less expensive.† As time value is not just about being paid for it, but also includes its

---

* DeSisto, R., *4 must-ask questions when choosing a grief-free CRM platform*, Medium, 2016.
† Dill, S., *Three Tips For Valuing Your Time As An Entrepreneur*, Forbes 2019.

allocation opportunities: what would be the long-term outcome of its allocation.

> *"But you must know that 48% of all salespeople never follow up and 64% of companies admit they do not have any organised way to nurture a lead.*
>
> *Follow up is one thing every company I have ever worked with agrees that, "We could do a better job with follow up." How do you get a customer back into your sales funnel? Don't feel bad if you aren't doing an excellent job of follow up because the reality is none of us are taught creative ways to follow up."*[*]

Grant Cardone wrote this in 2017. Since then the situation has improved and many CRM vendors and marketing scholars have helped the public to discuss Relational Marketing which ultimately is the real kernel of the CRM know-how.

For this reason, if we look at the resource-allocation strategy point of view, the decision about selecting a CRM solution may be crucial for many businesses. In this perspective, vendors that introduced entry-level solutions have created benefits to the industry helping companies to start with little then grow.

On one hand, the risk that companies, left alone just with entry-level CRM tools, may face is that they often struggle to identify the problems they meet: which of them are just tool's limitations and which of them are know-how impediments? People may develop the belief they are limitations of every CRM, and that a CRM tool is more a hassle than of any help. Entrepreneurs may become accustomed to cheap prices, and instead of wondering why such differences in price, they just develop low price (low value) expectations. On the other hand it is a human attitude and an entrepreneurial mission to seek resource savings. The industry commitment should be to enhance the culture around CRM beyond just the digital tools, it would help people in getting more confident and try experimenting in a more open way. We should all be involved in seeking ways to enhance the industry instead of levelling it to the bottom.

If the industry is capable of better supporting independent voices and more knowledgeable approaches for the benefit of everyone, the presence of low-cost solutions will be then more beneficial to everyone. And this enhanced know-how will overcome the issues created by cheap, very

---

[*] Cardone, G., *Do you know WHY you need a CRM?*, Medium, 2017.

convincing vendors who promote the idea of Do-It-Yourself with just a few dollars per month, leading to wrong assumptions the end users.

Buyers should also make an effort to educate themselves about the topic, the market trends and their own needs. When good providers meet buyers who know what they want, everyone works better and projects succeed more often. It can be complex to become knowledgeable about the whole perspective of CRM if you are not dedicated to it (isn't the same to everything?). Entrepreneurs and managers already have a lot to look after in their own businesses, developing in the first person a digital tool should be on their top priority or can they delegate it?

CRM Vendors and Platforms

Here we are going to list some of the most relevant vendors and their CRM solutions. To do it we will use the Gartner Magic Quadrant Report 2020 about CRM. We selected, in a totally arbitrary mode, just a few of them that we consider most relevant for the market as a benchmark. We do not endorse them; we simply believe they all have some good reasons before being so popular. We will add some tools not included in the Gartner research, a work we appreciate, even if we do not really always agree with their conclusion or with their selection of tools. It follows an extract from Gartner Magic Quadrant for the CRM Customer Engagement Center 2020.*

Microsoft

Microsoft is a Leader in this Magic Quadrant; the same as last year. It offers CEC capabilities via its Dynamics 365 Customer Service solution (v.9) and in its Dynamics 365 Customer Service Insights, Power Virtual Agents, and Power Automate applications. Collectively, these apps unite the standard functionalities of a customer service solution—case management, knowledge management and multiexperience engagement—with AI-driven insights built on a single platform that unifies tech stacks and customer data. Microsoft offers its service worldwide, mostly to enterprises. Consider Microsoft if you are looking to provide multichannel support for your front-office customer service teams, or if you are looking for a more standard back-office case management or ticketing system for internal or external service needs. Otherwise, consider it if the use of related apps such as Microsoft 365, Power BI, Power Apps, or other Dynamics 365 apps are key to your customer service strategy.

---

* https://www.gartner.com/en/documents/3991199/magic-quadrant-for-enterprise-low-code-application-platf.

Strengths

Advancing platform: The Dynamics 365 CEC offering builds on the same codebase as the Microsoft Power Platform, which is a low-code platform that spans Microsoft 365.

Intelligent customer service: One of Microsoft's focus areas is on bringing AI capabilities like Azure Cognitive Services, Microsoft Bot Framework and Power Virtual Agents together to provide more intelligent customer service experiences for both customers and agents.

Integration and automation: Dynamics 365 Customer Service provides extensive support for the integration of multiple line-of-business applications. Customer engagements are supported by a unified agent view and rich RPA capabilities for end-to-end customer service.

Cautions

Digital engagement capabilities: Microsoft has made strides over the past year to reduce dependency on third-party integration for digital channels, but the feature set is new and not market-tested. This year, Dynamics 365's digital engagement capabilities received the lowest scores out of all vendors evaluated.

Support team synergies: Reference customers reported that Microsoft appears to be siloed and resource-constrained between the Azure and Dynamics teams. Companies that are shortlisting Microsoft and expecting greater synergies between its offerings should fully investigate what these component capabilities actually bring.

Solution layering: Reference customers gave the Dynamics 365 solution layering a low score because of application lifecycle management practices for migration of customer solutions between test, UAT and production environments.

Oracle

Oracle is a Leader; the same as last year. For this Magic Quadrant, we evaluated Oracle CX Service—a set of customer service applications that is part of the Oracle CX suite. Reference customers identified Oracle as one of the three vendors most commonly mentioned by those looking for a customer service solution. Primary enhancements in the past year have been to channels, digital assistants and embedded service experiences. Oracle CX Service should be considered by B2C organizations that have complex processes and require strong integration capabilities. It is also used by B2B organizations, most notably in the high-tech and manufacturing industries. Oracle operates worldwide.

Strengths

Vision: Oracle demonstrates continuous delivery of innovations, with a focus on predictive service in the CEC market. Its channel proliferation and convergence, ability to connect visual experiences and commitment to digital customer service are leading edge.

Oracle Intelligent Advisor (OIA): OIA (previously known as Oracle Policy Automation or OPA), paired with strong integration capabilities, provides smart advice that determines and delivers the right decisions to its users with self-service and new conversational channels.

Knowledge management: Oracle offers one of the most scalable and functional knowledge management solutions among service suite vendors. In 2019, Oracle continued to innovate with an emphasis on how knowledge is consumed by both human and automated conversational agents.

Cautions

Licensing and contracts: Reference customers said that they found Oracle's license structure and matrix complex and their entitlements difficult to forecast. They also said that Oracle could be difficult to contract and negotiate with because its processes are stringent and the approval for contracts is lengthy.

Chatbot automation: Oracle scored low in the automation of engagement category in the reference customer survey. Clients admitted to finding the technical migration to the new Oracle Digital Assistant challenging.

Migration: When trying to migrate from Siebel CRM to Oracle Service Cloud, Gartner clients reported insufficient clarity of communication about how to do so, both from Oracle and its partners.

Salesforce

Salesforce is a Leader in this Magic Quadrant; the same as last year. About two-thirds (64%) of prospective CEC customers with whom Gartner has contact shortlisted Salesforce Service Cloud as their first, second or third choice (its nearest competitor in this regard was shortlisted by 35% of customers). Over the last 12 months, Salesforce has added more than 125 new features and enhancements to Service Cloud, including WhatsApp, real-time AI-based case classification, skills- based routing and next best action. Worldwide, both B2C and B2B midsize companies and large enterprises should consider Salesforce for its CEC solution.

Strengths

Vision: Salesforce's global presence, market impact and vision to transform customer service is unmatched so far by other vendors in this market.

Voice services: The introduction of Service Cloud Voice (general availability planned for 3Q20) will give customers the option to bring new, pre integrated voice services through Amazon Connect. This will be in addition to the vendor's ability to integrate with other contact center voice offerings.

Platform add-ons: Being part of the extensible Salesforce platform, complemented by the AppExchange marketplace, the Ignite customer innovation program and the Trailhead learning platform and community, helps Salesforce differentiate its Service Cloud product with more features and functions.

Cautions

Diffuse products: Customers continue to struggle with the lack of native integration, and with the architectural differences between the different Salesforce Clouds.

Inconsistent service providers: Service providers implementing Salesforce functionalities show inconsistent capabilities, which leads to troubled implementations and loss of agility in the speed of deployment.

Prices and contracts: Reference customers for Salesforce expressed concerns about high prices and vendor lock-in after integrating multiple Salesforce components or adding third-party components for industry-specific implementations, interactive voice response and telephony infrastructure.

Zendesk

Zendesk is a Leader in this Magic Quadrant; the same as last year. Zendesk Support is part of the Support Suite, which combines a customer communication hub strategy with engagement orchestration features to form the basis of the vendor's CEC application. Zendesk acquired Smooch, now Sunshine Conversations, a messaging platform for conversational business, and launched Zendesk Gather, a community experience product, and Zendesk Duet, a combined sales and service offering. Zendesk works globally, often with midsize customers and increasingly with enterprises. Consider Zendesk if you expect user adoption to be a particular challenge, if a SaaS-based application is the most suitable, or if an industry-specific solution is not essential.

Strengths

Innovation: Zendesk continues to innovate at a significant pace. It launched several key products and features in 2019 like Zendesk Duet, Gather and Sunshine Conversations.

Easy to use: Reference customers continue to appreciate the ease of use of the product and find benefit in the fast time to value and agility it delivers to customers.

Public cloud: Zendesk offers a public cloud solution, Zendesk Sunshine, with an extensive application ecosystem. Its app marketplace offers over 950 easily added apps.

Cautions

Enterprise customers: Zendesk has made strides toward meeting the needs of true enterprise customers but is still continuing to develop its solution. Reference customers said that the solution is inconsistent, particularly when it comes to stability and quality.

Need for complexity: Zendesk's focus on simplicity has resulted in large customer service centers finding its interface less intuitive when trying to manage significant numbers of advisors. Only a small percentage of Zendesk's customers have 500 or more seats.

Pricing and contracts: Zendesk's complex and inflexible pricing and contract options concern Gartner's enterprise clients.

SugarCRM

SugarCRM is a Niche Player in this Magic Quadrant; the same as last year. Its primary CEC solution is Sugar Serve, part of the Winter '20 release, which was introduced for the first time mid-2019 as a stand-alone offering, breaking out of Sugar Enterprise. SugarCRM strengthened its ecosystem portfolio with integrations with the likes of Genesys, 8x8 and Amazon Connect to enhance its customer service proposition. Seventy-five percent of Sugar Serve customers are from the Americas and 16% from EMEA. Consider SugarCRM if you represent a midsize support organization looking for a capable customer engagement solution, or if you are already using, or planning to deploy, sales automation.

Strengths

Simple to use: SugarCRM is easily configured and customized. No special training or proprietary scripting languages are needed to achieve results.

Integration: SugarCRM demonstrates focus on the ability to integrate with contact center platforms and legacy contact center environment technology.

Customer support: Reference customers showed consistent satisfaction with the vendor and its dedication to its customers during deployment.

Cautions

Growing pains: Sugar Serve is a young solution that needs to be expanded, as currently several gaps can be identified in digital engagement and case management capabilities.

Small marketplace: SugarCRM's application marketplace offers very few technology partner solutions. Sugar Enterprise will not meet the needs of customers that require a robust, self-service-based CRM application ecosystem, as provided by some other CEC competitors.

Customer support: Reference customers reported that SugarCRM could improve its capabilities for maintenance and customer support.

Zendesk Sell

We would like to clarify that Gartner only considered Zendesk Support and, strangely enough, they didn't write one single word about Zendesk Sell (previously named Future Simple, then PipeJump and lastly as Base), the sales-oriented CRM that the company bought in 2018. Base CRM was a Polish-born, Californian-established company that has been recognised by many publications for its intuitiveness, mobility and clean design. In

February 2013, Base was recognised by Forbes as one of 10 Mobile Apps to Organise Your Business. In October 2012, Fortune positioned Base as the next major disruptor in the CRM space.*

Zendesk Sell has become then a powerful platform that strongly benefits from its full integration within the impressive Zendesk ecosystem.

Strengths

Direct native integration with a powerful customer support (Zendesk Support) tool and a strong cloud app for omni-channel conversational platform (Sunshine). Great looking UI, light and professional.

Limitations

The CRM is well designed but lacks of some basic tools in the data management, it may imply users have to download data in csv files to manage bulk alterations. UI with some arguable choices in terms of information rendering.

Pipedrive CRM

This tool has been developed with business-to-business sales process management in mind. The Estonian-born New York-headquartered company has quite powerful marketing strategy that enable its tremendous growth. This is now one of the most appreciated CRM tools among start-ups and micro- and small business.

Pipedrive is rated as the most popular CRM and awarded as the most easy-to-use solution for salespeople. It is specifically designed to help SMBs efficiently manage their sales processes. The company has been recognised as the "Best Overall CRM Solution in 2020" by MarTech Breakthrough[†] and "Easiest to Use CRM" by Motley Fool.[‡] Since 2018, Pipedrive has been included in the highly competitive Forbes Cloud 100 list, the definitive ranking of the top hundred private cloud companies in the world, published by Forbes.[§] Probably the most relevant innovation that Pipedrive has introduced to the market is the Visual Sales Pipeline Management that is considered to

* Savitz, E., *Revolution: A New Era In Software For Small Businesses*, Forbes 2012.
† https://martechbreakthrough.com/2020-winners/.
‡ Cision, PRNEWSWIRE, *Pipedrive Awarded "Easiest to Use" CRM by The Motley Fool*, 2020.
§ Madiya, N., *Pipedrive Reserves Its Place Again In The List of 2020 Forbes Cloud 100*, https://emergingcloudtech.com, 2020.

be its core and the most user friendly approach to sales process management.* Another relevant innovation relies on its embedded Activity Based Selling methodology, which was developed to enhance the salespeople day-to-day routine and engaging them in their commitment.

Strengths

Intuitive UX, easy to use visual pipelines settings, fully integrated with hundreds of solutions, open API for developers.

Limitations

While its core feature work fine, many collateral features are not as good as its core, it lacks of a master control: settings of users, features, functions and integrations must be done one by one.

HubSpot

The third relevant player that Gartner didn't include is the Cambridge (MA)-based vendor, HubSpot. Its solution, born as a marketing automation is still strongly focused on the leads generation stage. Established in 2006, the company has grown solidly. Since 2012 it has made progress and the suite is now stable and stronger. Probably not as "easy to use" as someone still labelling it, but in its focus on online marketing and leads generation, it has won a solid position in the industry.

HubSpot has been described as unique because it strives to provide its customers with an all-in-one approach. A 2012 review of *CRMSearch* said HubSpot was not the best business solution in each category, but that, taken as a whole, it was the best "marketing solution" that combined many tools into one package.

Strengths

The sophistication of its Call to Action tool, its broader control of the leads journey and content management, what has been described as Inbound Marketing.

---

* https://tech.co/crm-software/crm-best-salesforce-alternatives.

Limitations

Described as more breadth than depth, is reported very complex to set and run and its pricing is also considered a premium positioning.

CRM Platforms Summary

In the Gartner report, the majority of vendors are mainly focused on the corporate market, while medium-sized companies may find them a bit less right for them, owing to their complexity and the impact of those tools on small businesses, their application is a strong business decision. Gartner also included some tools better balanced for medium enterprises, probably none for small businesses.

An approach would be to analyse those tools as reference of the market, and after clarifying the magnitude of the project and the subtleties of the business, entering into an effort/benefit evaluation stage with care, the outcome would be a considered selection of tools that may fit better the organisational requirements.

Dynamics is a debated CRM from the brand of Seattle. Its power is beyond question as well as its strong capability to work on the marketing side, especially in business-to-consumer frameworks. To whom who loves the vendor Dynamics is a clear way to go, when the business magnitude is big enough to sustain this complexity and benefit of it. Clients report a high complexity in the set-up and probably overall a not quite easy-to-use system; the use in B2B seems less remarkable as salespeople management has been reported less stable than clients would expect it.

Oracle and Salesforce are two of the most advanced and widely used CRMs for the corporate segment. This kind of tools require a substantial investment in design and implementation, in some way they are quite flexible to operate in B2B and B2C business models but their best return is probably on B2C as it is a model where fragemented, multiple interaction with thousands of contacts to lead them across complex contents and marketing messages really requires a powerful platform. Users are reporting the need of a long learning curve before to become productive.

SugarCRM, Zendesk and HubSpot are more focused on the midsized enterprise market and they tend to be omni-comprehensive tools. Even though Zendesk and HubSpot developed (or bought) separate apps for CRM and they can run either independently or integrated into their ecosystems, while SugarCRM is mainly a strong CRM platform with capabilities of flexibility into a structured framework. Since HubSpot has been ditched from Salesforce as their preferred marketing automation, they are actually proposing the CRM as a entry level freeware solution, their marketing strategy aimed to attract clients has been quite successful.

Pipedrive is a completely different tool. The market main focus was since the beginning on small and micro-businesses; lately also midsized companies are started using it benefitting by the laser-focused approach on sales process management for B2B. For a tool positioned in the entry-level segment Pipedrive shows a quite good powerful core system and a plethora of integrated, third parties solutions - its ecosystem. The segment where Pipedrive sits is notoriously crowded, and becoming relevant among so many competitors is a remarkable achievement. In this segment, many solutions lack investments to become good enough or their companies often may lack vision, therefore they tend to remain small software houses with a single product. Even worse, many vendors risk developing just "another digital tool" with few or no differentiation idea on what pain they really want to solve: in the absence of a specific mission-oriented proposal they end up staying in limbo.

Some vendors are also trying to bridge the gap between their entry-level segment and their more complex solutions aimed to bigger businesses. It will be great if that happens, supporting the market with more qualified proposals instead of a few huge brands and too many dwarves. The problems for long established vendors is to offer good enough solutions at right prices for mid size companies when they are more comfortable serving corporations. In this sense some relatively new entry as Zendesk Sell or Pipedrive or even HubSpot could play a relevant role in this area.

Low-Code Platforms

Low-code development platform is an application that provides the Graphical User Interface for programming and thereby develops the code at a fastest rate, reducing the programming efforts. Some platforms are also pretty good for a quick deployment. The market appears healthy; the number of vendors continues to grow, corresponding with increasing demand. It is a mission impossible to analyse even a portion of so many proposals available in the market. We limited the analysis to the most relevant excluding, sorry for that, many that probably are also valuable, at least we wanted to propose an overview and a benchmark. Low code is a relatively new approach in developing solutions of any kind. Well beyond CRM tools, its value relies on the speeding up of the development, reducing the time enabling even non developers to control the logic and features, workflows and processes, avoiding the need to intervene at the deep code level every time. The benefit of using low coding can be frustrated by vendors that are not fully committed to supporting standard procedures or even standard languages (SQL). Their databases should be fully relational, and the documentation clear and complete. One of the worst experiences a company can encounter when testing a low-code tech solution is to discover only when already locked-in by the vendor that the solution doesn't properly run SQL commands or that some other routine but slightly more complex task can't be performed inside the platform. For this reason, deciding carefully on the vendor definitely matters. All the security certifications should be in place.* The following is an extract from Gartner Magic Quadrant for Enterprise Low-Code Application Platforms 2020.†

Appian

Appian offers low-code app building, rich multiexperience capabilities, business process orchestration, automated decisioning, AI/ML and RPA. The platform focuses on complex processes such as end-to-end case management and other applications requiring sophisticated automation, rules and analytics. Its technological differentiators include full-stack automation capabilities, prebuilt no-code integration with various AI services, and end-to-end life cycle support for DevOps. Appian has operations in every major world region, with a focus on large enterprises. Its 2020 roadmap includes enhancements to AI-service integration, DevOps capabilities, RPA and expanded AI support for application development.

Strengths

Product: At the core of Appian's LCAP strength is its rich process-driven application development. Appian's ability to offer a complete stack of low-code automation tooling that can handle complex workflows, business rules and case management along with RPA is a key differentiator. Added to that, it offers low-code tools to build multiexperience apps to enable customer and employee experiences.

Market understanding: Appian brings in a complete end-to-end solution for its customers by enabling low-code capabilities to build business applications, perform complex process orchestration, and automate

---

* Software Testing Help, *10 Best Low-Code Development Platforms In 2021*, November 2021 (https://www.softwaretestinghelp.com/low-code-development-platforms/).

† https://www.gartner.com/en/documents/3985947/magic-quadrant-for-the-crm-customer-engagement-center

routine repetitive tasks with RPA. Customers looking for a full-stack automation platform should consider Appian's LCAP.

Overall viability: In a crowded market with many small, privately owned vendors, Appian stands out as a stable, publicly traded company with a focus on low-code technology. Although smaller than many of its competitors, Appian has many enterprise customers and government agencies running its platform, which should ensure its long-term viability in this market.

Cautions

Application development: Some of Gartner's Peer Insight reviewers found that Appian's low-code development product is more suitable for professional developers. Appian's proprietary expression and scripting language is typically an inhibitor for "citizen developers" building algorithmic expressions. Although Appian has built some collaborative features to support multiple personas—including both citizen and pro developers—Gartner has not yet seen much adoption.

Sales execution and pricing: Appian pricing has been observed as highly variable in Gartner inquiries. Recently, the vendor has made some changes with a simplified basic subscription model, an annual "Quick Start License" and other options that may allay customer concerns in future.

Business model: Appian has a high proportion of professional services revenue associated with its LCAP business. While some of these services are likely legacy business process reengineering consulting, and others related to large projects associated with its targeting of larger enterprises, the proportion of services to product revenue implies more specialist developer requirements.

Oracle (Visual Builder)

Visual Builder product is mainly focused on professional developers customizing Oracle SaaS products for multiexperience, as well as consumers of the wider Oracle Integration Cloud stack. Visual Builder provides services access and coordination with a multiexperience front end. Oracle's vision is of a unified DevOps and low-code stack, released recently as Visual Builder Platform.

Strengths

Overall viability: Oracle is a large and successful DBMS and SaaS vendor. The latter increasingly relies on Visual Builder as the primary development and extension mechanism, and Oracle SaaS is a major growth engine for Oracle. Therefore, Visual Builder will be increasingly employed for Oracle SaaS development and customization, and potentially for those customers constructing new SaaS.

Product: Visual Builder includes the Oracle JET engine for mobile and web development, and provides ready access to multiexperience UIs. The paradigm of event-driven "action chains" to provide advanced user experiences, on top of a full REST API and catalog access, alongside developer automation tooling (including DevOps and test-case generation) is instrumental in Oracle's Visionary placement in this Magic Quadrant.

Pricing: Almost uniquely among the vendors presented in this Magic Quadrant, Oracle's pricing for Visual Builder is resource-based and therefore dependent only on consumption—with no dependency on user counts or other metrics that can discourage adoption. This makes Visual Builder much more accessible for new use cases

Cautions

Market understanding: Oracle's policy of separating out specialist products for standard LCAP functions (such as business processes and often integrations) means that Visual Builder customers need to learn and license additional components for these capabilities. Indeed, the majority of Visual Builder users acquire it as a component of Oracle Integration Cloud (which itself is not an LCAP). This puts Visual Builder into the category of more specialist tooling compared with the more multifunction offerings that increasingly are embedding those capabilities.

Marketing execution: Oracle does not make much effort to market Visual Builder. Its recent release of Visual Builder Platform was communicated as a blog post, and Gartner inquiries for it are rare. So while Oracle appears to recognize the vision of SaaS plus PaaS, it seems reticent to promote itself in this area. It also fails to market the advantages and differences of its two separate LCAPs (see also Oracle APEX), likely causing reduced adoption.

Platform ecosystem: Visual Builder provides easy component access to its business objects and Oracle SaaS services, but Oracle does not promote a rich third-party ecosystem for its customers and partners to market to and share. This means that, despite an advantageous pricing model and multiexperience capabilities, Oracle Visual Builder provides a less-rich target audience for potential OEMs.

FileMaker

Gartner didn't take into consideration FileMaker, the Apple platform for low coding.

The platform displays quick find, quick reports and customisable themes for the ease of developers. Other features include, but are not limited to, highlighted script errors, ESS adapter, external SQL data connection and more.

Pre-built templates help businesses to build a robust app for internal use to manage assets and data in one place. Secure data and full supervision of the admin on users' roles and permissions restrict access to controlled data as well as built-in reports, charts, dashboards and built-in reports. Filemaker was strong since the 1990s' when it established a great positioning in a market that was not quite born yet. Later the solution lost a bit of grip, being reported slow when used in big project, with online apps. Recently it appears to fix the main issues but is not anymore so in-vogue for developers, they actually created a focused solution-provider network capable to support business in adopting this tool. It may be a good thing, but while its pricing remain premium also its adoption may be more for a niche. Built-in reports, charts, dashboards and built-in reports.

Strengths

Highly flexibility in a fully developed framework. Overall a great tool, probably also thanks to its long presence in the market.

Limitations

Limited interoperability that requires quite costly solutions, high level of specialised skills involved in its set-up and maintenance.

Visual Lansa

This platform is proposed as a way to build better, build faster any application for IT teams and software developers to reduce the human work (hire less) and reduce time. They claim to interpret the digital transformation for business with a powerful approach at a quite decent pricing.

> *Digital transformation: Transform your manual and paper-based processes into web, mobile, cloud, and desktop applications for better efficiency, productivity, and data accuracy.*
> *Go mobile: Quickly mobile-enable the parts of your business that need remote access to business-critical information. Enable IT to reduce costs and improve the bottom line.*
> *Deploy anywhere: The flexibility to deploy to an IBM i or Windows server, or, take your apps to the cloud anytime for better agility and elasticity. Improve availability while cutting operational costs.**

Strengths

Interesting balance cost/performance, visual high control of the environment. Part of a big ecosystem.

Limitations

Probably a solution which still under development, some user found the Debugger not fully useful and documentation little bit short. The matter is: learn Lowcode platform is a job itself.

Bubble

The small company is going big. Born as a small solution around front-end application Bubble has got $100 M to grow in 2021. They claim to have created a new programming language based on visual no-code. For web app bubble can be a solution to watch in the near future. It is now pretty good to build faster MVP and testing apps.

---

* Lansa.com, Company's promotion.

Strengths

Easy to learn, fast to put in place, supports webpage creation and their deployment live. Pricing really affordable.

Limitations

After 9 years still a solution "on-development". In need of strong development.

Ninox

Born as cloud database positioned on the lower market pricing and for long time struggling with its own management culture, this small company seems about to restart its way to grow. Thanks to a management change that probably matters on its culture rebuilding and from that point to its whole market presence, Ninox is offering quite useful tools to easy develop simple process management applications.

Strengths

Easy to set up, really really low cost. About to change radically, hence probably more benefit to come.

Limitations

No relational database, limited rendering capabilities, in need of great investment to build reliability, performance and usefulness.

Low-Code Platform Summary

We listed some relevant vendors according to the Gartner Magic Quadrant Report 2020 about low-code platforms. Our selection is totally arbitrary, mainly for a market benchmark. We also listed some platforms, out of the Gatner Report that can't be fully comprehensive, to provide an better overview of possible solutions that enable medium size enterprise in creating their own CRM tool and more.

In some cases, even small companies could benefit from developing a bespoke solution when their needs are not fully covered by existing ready-to-use platforms and/or if their pricing can be a deterrent. Low-code platforms may simplify, accelerate and reduce costs of app development, which is interesting either for business people to reduce IT dependence, as well as for IT departments to enhance productivity. The potential of low-code development can be impressive and we are just at its early stage of market adoption.

Conclusion of the Chapter and the Book

In this chapter, we reported reviews of solutions available in the market with some considerations on our side but mainly relying on the publicly available ones. The intention was to report an overview that everyone can use for arranging a deeper investigation, being of the belief that every organisation should analyse and verify carefully the best possible solution under their own requirements and expectations.

The purpose of this chapter, was to provide a different perspective beyond just the CRM solution vendors, the purpose of this book was to give everyone, with a special care to non-tech business people, a completely different view around CRM.

We hope to have been able to contribute to readers' enhancement also enjoying you all, developing a practice guide for organisations, entrepreneurs and managers who prepare themselves for a CRM migration.

As previously mentioned, no company exists without a CRM.

Hence, adopting a solution that helps to avoid the hazards of memory loss, paper alight or spreadsheet mess is a challenge to the organisational way of manage relationships. For this reason, we left the discussion over tools to a minimum. We strongly believe that implementing a digital tool has no value if the organisation doesn't prepare it based on its own strategic view. Moreover, implementing a tool under urgency, shortcutting the complex decision-making process, is probably among the most common reasons for such a high CRM project failure rate.

With this book we wanted help organisations and entrepreneurs in developing a better approach to their CRM projects, thereby helping everyone to work better.

Index

Printed in the United States
by Baker & Taylor Publisher Services